Prepublication Reviews

"In a time dominated by an overwhelming influx of information, paired with the rapid evolution of artificial intelligence, today's leaders face the challenge of staying informed while often losing touch with their own inner wisdom. In this insightful book, Greg Stebbins offers a timely and transformative reminder of the power of reconnecting with our heart-centered wisdom.

"Stebbins takes readers on an enriching journey of self-discovery, encouraging practices like self-empathy, self-compassion, and self-love. Through this process, he lays the foundation for a deeper understanding of oneself, which serves as the cornerstone for meaningful relationships with others. The book goes beyond theory, providing a practical framework to help leaders cultivate trust, compassion, and authentic connection within their teams and organizations.

"This book is an essential read for leaders of today and tomorrow, as well as for anyone seeking to align with their heart's wisdom in both personal and professional spheres. It is a compelling guide for fostering a culture of empathy and genuine understanding in a fast-paced, information-saturated world."

Matthew Heim, Ph.D. – United States
Author of *Breaking the Musashi Code:*
Transcending Competition Through Visionary Strategy

"Gregory Stebbins, Ed.D., is not just an insightful author and visionary leader — he's also a dear friend whose presence and wisdom I deeply value. His book, *Wise Leadership: Embracing Our Heart's Wisdom,* is a masterful reflection of his ability to combine the transformative power of love, wisdom, and self-loving into a guide for conscious leadership. Gregory shows us that true leadership starts within — by nurturing self-compassion and self-awareness, we create the foundation to lead others with authenticity and integrity. His understanding of our heart's quiet wisdom inspires a deeper connection to ourselves and those we serve. Knowing Gregory, this book is a mirror of his life's work and his commitment to fostering a world where self-loving, love, and wisdom of our heart are central to meaningful leadership and shared humanity."

Jsu Garcia – Global Citizen
Author, *The Love of a Master*

"I read this book right after watching the memorial service for President Carter. If we need an example of wise leadership, he is one of the best in recent times. One of the characteristics pointed out by Carter's grandson was that his grandfather was the same person with whoever he met — a head of state, a family member, or a poor African villager. He loved and respected each one. The confidence to hold that level of internal integrity is one of the hallmarks of wisdom. It also gave him the courage to make decisions that he knew would be unpopular, but that were right in the long run.

"That is what *Wise Leadership: Embracing Our Heart's Wisdom* calls us to, and Greg Stebbins lays out a path to develop this level of integrity within ourselves. It has always been important, but in our current state of climate change, political polarization and conflict, increased concentration of wealth, AI, and every form of media vying for our attention it is becoming critical. It takes tremendous will to find our own grounding, to honor our own experience, to be authentic within ourselves and the same person with everyone else. This book reminds us that it is doable, brings joy, and positively affects others we may never know. If you are called to this kind of leadership, *Wise Leadership: Embracing Our Heart's Wisdom,* by Gregory Stebbins, can be a wonderful companion."

Dr. Mary Emeny – Global Citizen
Founding Member Habitat for Humanity International

"It is both an Honor and Pleasure to express my personal and professional relationship with Dr Gregory Stebbins. He has been my mentor and coach for more than 46 years. As a Female Pilot, when we met up in 1979, it was my heart's Desire to become an Airline Pilot and fly Jumbo Jets all over the world. His "Yes You Can" became my North Star.

"For him, it was a small task; for me, it was a giant mountain. With his extraordinary intelligence, innate intuition, loving heart, and Spirit, Greg understood how to follow and guide toward that "North Star." He can help you re-calibrate your inner compass, encourage you, and influence you. I've often asked him to write down what he does. *Wise Leadership: Embracing Our Heart's Wisdom* does just that.

"Through his experiences, he reveals how to reframe your past and bring your future into focus, thus making it a reality. His tools guide you, and he reminds you to never forget your own inner "True North." He gives you a good direction to get the results that your heart desires in life. He reveals course corrections, always reminding one that goals, too, have challenges along the way.

"I am proud to say I flew Jumbo Jet's all around the world."

Kim Calvin – United States
Retired Airline Pilot

"Traditional leadership literature often prioritizes logic and control, overlooking the importance of intuition and authenticity. In contrast, Dr. Gregory Stebbins emphasizes the essential role of inner reflection and connecting with "the wisdom of our heart" for today's leaders. This book is a must-read for all leaders, offering a powerful reminder to ground themselves in hope, love, and authenticity amidst the fast-paced changes of the modern world."

Parineeta Bartakke - India
Director – Bartakke Electrofab Pvt. Ltd

"I found *Wise Leadership: Embracing Our Heart's Wisdom* by Dr. Gregory Stebbins to be a profound and timely guide that masterfully bridges the gap between leadership effectiveness and heart-centered wisdom. As I read, I discovered how authentic leadership transcends mere data and skills, as Stebbins guided me to access my inner compass that's often drowned out by organizational noise.

"The book's exploration of head, hunch, and heart offered me a refreshing perspective on authentic leadership that's both practical and profoundly transformative. What touched me most is that Stebbins doesn't just articulate insights — I experienced a kind of transmission that shifted me into a place of stillness and deeper listening to my heart's wisdom. Reading this valuable offering, I found it to be a soul-nourishing contribution to wisdom-based leadership that honors our own hearts and those of the people we lead and serve. For me, it was a must-read journey into making decisions that are not just smart but truly wise — highly recommended."

Gregory Vahanian – United States
Transformational Life Coach, Author,
and Speaker at Gregory Vahanian Coaching

"In a world consumed with information overload and confusion, going still to listen to our heart might seem preposterous. The deep-seated belief that leadership is just about efficiency alone has derailed many talented individuals with high IQ/EQ scores. Dr Stebbins brilliantly proposes multi-brain integration in his pioneering book *Wise Leadership: Embracing Our Heart's Wisdom* to help leaders become effective leaders, not just productive high achievers. His elegant prose helps us understand complex concepts and invites us to move from insight to impact. This book is a timely work that will — undoubtedly — revolutionise how leadership is understood and taught in many business schools worldwide".

Dr. Marcos Cajina Heinzkill – Global Citizen
Founder and President of Renewal.
10 consecutive year recipient of the *Teaching Excellence*
***Award and Lifelong Learning Excellence* at the**
IE Business School-Executive Education

"The book *Wise Leadership: Embracing Our Heart's Wisdom* by Greg Stebbins, Ed.D., is a compact and thought-provoking examination of an aspect of leadership that deserves more attention than it has traditionally been given. This aspect is the need for decision-makers to turn inward before making certain critical decisions to ensure that moral and ethical considerations are accounted for. Dr. Stebbins refers to this as listening to the "Heart's Wisdom."

"Among the wisdom-related topics addressed in the book are: (i) the differences between "wisdom" and "information" (an all-important distinction in our age of non-stop information streaming), (ii) how "wisdom" has been thought of from the time of the ancient Greeks to the present, and (iii) techniques leaders can use to best access the wisdom that is inherent within them.

"Dr. Stebbins is a recognized expert in the field of practical "how to do" leadership and his latest book should be a valuable addition to this field. The book should be helpful to leaders of all levels of experience and will be especially valuable to beginning or emerging leaders. During my 30-plus years of serving Florida Power & Light Company in various managerial positions, the training I received during that time period did not address the main topic of this book. Looking back, I can think of at least several instances in which this knowledge would have been helpful."

Dr. Steven Sim – United States
Director of Resource Planning (retired),
Florida Power & Light Company.

"As the world casts about to define the leadership its needs for the post-knowledge economy, this book offers an answer anchored in an essentially human capacity: wisdom of our heart. Greg writes: "Wisdom fundamentally means discernment — the ability to see situations, relationships, and challenges for what they more deeply are." The ability to see both clearly *and* deeply is not a technical skill, but emerges from an inner knowing that we cultivate through living and leading with integrity: with the whole of oneself, unfragmented, unbroken, de-compartmentalized, and anchored confidently in accep-tance and gratitude. Greg reminds us that people have always possessed this capacity, ready to guide us in shaping our future, and we still do.

"This book is a contemplation whose depth matches that of its topic in the warmly elicited clarity it brings to big concepts like courage, self-loving, empathy, authenticity, resonance, and transcendence. I can't wait for my students to read it. It will challenge, inspire, and reassure them all simultaneously."

Jody Ono – Global Citizen
Hitotsubashi University Business School, School of
International Corporate Strategy, Tokyo, Japan

"This book fully showcases Dr. Stebbins's decades of coaching high-level executives and developing educational programs for highly successful leaders. As someone who has impressively walked this path of wise leadership, he speaks not only from head to head but also from heart to heart.

"He takes concepts that might be described as complex at best and provides practical approaches, tools, and techniques to not only understand them but to practice and master them.

"A respected pioneer in heart-centered leadership, Stebbins has boldly gone where few have gone before. He was among the first to speak openly about wisdom, as contrasted with intelligence, in leadership and to describe the role of loving as a component of leading."

Laren Bright – United States

"While reading Greg Stebbins's *Wise Leadership: Embracing Our Heart's Wisdom,* I was struck by its common-sense approach and his impressive interconnectivity of focused thoughts right from the "Simple but Not Easy" introduction, which continued throughout the book. For me, Chapter 5's "Small Moments of Pause" reaffirmed my belief that we all need to think before we speak or act, and Chapter 8's emphasis on cultivating gratitude and presence focused on appreciating and celebrating even small wins in our behavior, performance, and communication. It was a reminder of the importance of leading people with mutually clear expectations - a focus in Chapter 9 that encourages problem-solving, resolution, fairness, and consistency. Dr.

Stebbins has indeed authored and offers "Words of Heartfelt Wisdom" that will resonate with each reader and cause them to pause, practice, cultivate, and encourage those they lead to "Lead with Your Heart!"

Alan A. Malinchak – United States
CEO, Eclat Transitions LLC and Chief Learning Officer (Retired)

"The vision and foundation, combined with the simplicity, use of examples, reflections, and tools presented, make Greg's book a profound expander of consciousness about what it means to lead and how to be a leader. He introduces the pillars of intellectual knowledge, emotional intelligence, and intuition in a way that both makes sense and inspires action.

"What struck me the most was how he discussed the fears associated with listening to and following our hearts' voices. We often avoid this out of insecurity, but Greg explains it so clearly and practically that it feels natural to begin trusting this process. I love the idea of intentional listening and how being present holds the key.

"This book isn't just a method for better leadership — it's a summons to become a better human being. Reading it helped me become more aware, connected, and motivated to apply what I've learned personally and professionally."

Gustavo Vieira – Brazil
Managing Partner and Design Lead at Livework Studio

"Dr. Greg's book brings you on an adventure where your heart rejoices, your spirits sing, and your nervous brain relaxes with deep contentment. You will find yourself reading something boldly unique yet familiar, as if you may have already known it long ago. As we take shape in the mother's womb, first comes our heart, then the brain. He reminds us that each pump in our heart produces strong electromagnetic waves that impact our brains and the people around us. As a result, our ability as leaders to protect and harness the power of our hearts to lead becomes critical. In a logic-first world, the environment and social structure tend to encourage us to seek validation from outside. As a result, we hear "narcissism" rising. Heart, on the other hand, talks to us in silence or small voices (intuition) and encourages us to seek validation from within and know that our contribution to the world is not our status, but our existence with each heartbeat "lub-dub" "lub-dub" "lub-dub..." and a simple practice of self-love. Then comes the balance. He pointed out that our ability to stay in a dynamic "middle way" to balance deep empathy and professional boundaries is an important practice of sustainability. The book then concludes that our heart is where our home is, always warm, alive, and welcoming. A leader who listens to our heart's wisdom is never alone, always loving, and always loved."

Dr. Jiani Wu – Global Citizen
Founder of MAGICademy "Embrace Your MAGIC Within"

"If you only read one leadership book this year, let it be *Wise Leadership: Embracing Our Heart's Wisdom*. In the age of Artificial Intelligence and rapidly advancing technology, Dr. Stebbins is calling all of us leaders to go back to our hearts, the quiet compass that exists within each of us and that can guide us toward wise decisions and superior outcomes. He encourages us, in a kind and gentle way, to overcome the fear of listening to our hearts and to develop the courage to lead with emotions, self-empathy, and self-loving. This is a very timely book that leaders will greatly benefit from applying its wisdom in their daily actions."

Dr. Amer Kaissi – United States
Professor, Executive Coach, and Professional Speaker
Trinity University & Amer Kaissi Group
Author - *Humbitious: The Power of Low-Ego,*
High-Drive Leadership

"Greg leads us into a territory that we might intuitively know is true, yet don't quite know how to awaken to it within ourselves. The territory of our heart's wisdom, complete with its expressions of purpose, compassion, authenticity, and love. He presents the key themes with bold, almost poetic practicality. Then he lays out a banquet of different practices that we can choose from, each encouraging and enabling us to make that territory our most welcoming home base within — and the greatest feature of our leadership.

"As a guide, Greg more than succeeds in informing, inspiring, and empowering us to find our way home to our true selves as leaders at work, at home, and in life. As he does so, it's clearly evident that he practices what he proclaims; his life as a leader and his experience as a leadership coach are evident on every page. We can easily trust that the potentialities and the opportunities he lays before us are indeed inherent in each of us, transforming the power of our leadership as they deepen our trust in ourselves."

William C. Miller – Global Citizen
Author of *Flash of Brilliance: Inspiring Creativity*
***Where You Work* and Co-author of**
Perennial Wisdom of the Conscious Innovator

"How refreshing!

"In his latest book, Dr. Stebbins advocates fully embracing our Heart as a pathway to Leadership. He suggests shifting focus to one's inner wisdom, which he calls a "Quiet Compass." He encourages listening more and speaking less, living and working authentically from our heart.

"This new book presents a genuinely revolutionary approach, urging us to lead with our hearts while highlighting care, compassion, and discernment. It provides various specific methods, such as contemplation and stillness, to connect with the inner wisdom that dwells within each of us, awaiting discovery.

"In my fifty years of ministry, I have often observed leaders becoming fixated on asserting their authority and self-importance through various means. They focused on specific outward goals as their mission, attempting to fulfill their personal agendas while completely neglecting the needs of those they led.

"If a Golden Age for humanity is indeed to emerge, it will arise among those who seek the Wisdom of Our Heart, promote community and synergy, and trust in and empower others. As someone with deep faith, I eagerly anticipate the coming years when Heart's Wisdom becomes the normative 'quiet compass' across business, law, education, health care, and all human interactions."

Rev. Penelope Townsend Bright, MSS – United States

"Wise Leadership: Embracing the Heart's Wisdom is a gripping and transformational read that redefines 21st-century leadership and anchors it in love, wisdom, and authenticity. As the world faces information overload and the exponential growth of artificial intelligence, Dr. Greg Stebbins calls on leaders to move forward from power-centric models of authority, charisma, and control. Instead, he provides a way inward to wisdom and heart-based leadership. Focusing on self-empathy, self-compassion, and self-awareness, Stebbins "reminds readers that the tools they need to lead with purpose and integrity already lie within them." The obstacle, he argues, is to find our way to our hearts by hearing, trusting, and developing the conviction to act from this well of being.

"This book teaches wisdom as something that transcends data or information, applying wisdom as an art of emotional reasoning, intuition, and integrity. Through practical methods intended to create trust, compassion, and presence, Stebbins offers leaders the tools to navigate complexity with discernment while building cultures of openness, accountability, and authenticity. His teachings combine ancient wisdom with modern leadership best practices, and he moves past the conventional reliance on logic and control to an approach that recognizes the totality of our being, balancing the mind, the heart, and the gut. Stebbins presents in our hyper-driven, bifurcated, knee-jerk world a blueprint for transformation that speaks to the hearts of leaders everywhere: the concept that the path to meaning for us all begins with the innate wisdom of our heart and proceeds from there to the emergence of a more compassionate future."

Lynn Cirillo – United States

"Greg Stebbins brilliantly bridges the gap between conventional leadership and the deeper wisdom we all possess but rarely access. In an era where leaders face crippling complexity, information overload, and an all-consuming AI revolution, this transformative guide reveals that our greatest power lies in going within. Through the chambers of the heart and the wisdom of the soul, Stebbins masterfully guides us to our True Power — showing us how to lead with intuition, authenticity, and deep purpose. Moving beyond mere efficiency and productivity, he illuminates how self-empathy, gratitude and heart-centered wisdom can transform our leadership presence. In a world drowning in data but starving for wisdom, Stebbins offers a profound pathway to accessing the extraordinary wisdom that lies within each of us, proving that our most powerful leadership advantage comes not from external knowledge but from embracing our full humanity and connecting with our soul's deeper purpose."

Rúna Bouius – Global Citizen
Founder of the True Power Institute,
TruePower Leadership Catalyst

Gregory
Stebbins Ed.D.

WISE LEADERSHIP

Embracing
Our Heart's
Wisdom

Author Online!

For seminars and more resources,
visit the PeopleSavvy website at

www.peoplesavvy.com

Published by:
Savvy Books
772 Element Way, Suite 405
Ashwaubenon, WI 54304
Email: info@savvybooks.com

ISBN: 978-1-887152-11-2

First Edition 2025

Cover and Interior Design: Creative Publishing Book Design

Acknowledgments

In 2018, I had the honor of being invited to join the Conscious Leadership Guild (CLG) as one of its Inaugural Members. Founded that same year, the CLG is a professional membership organization dedicated to supporting its members in developing and refining their conscious leadership skills. It represents a vibrant, growing community of individuals committed to leading with intention, integrity, and love.

How the Guild Began

The journey of the Conscious Leadership Guild began with a vision shared by a diverse group of executives, consultants, and academics. This group came together during a Conscious Leadership Congress retreat, where they explored the power and potential of conscious leadership. Inspired by the insights and connections fostered during the retreat, these pioneers collaborated to create a formal organization to nurture and expand this work. The Guild was officially incorporated in California and, in 2020, achieved non-profit status from the IRS.

The Guild's Purpose and Vision

At its core, the Guild exists to help its members strengthen their competency and consciousness, with the ultimate goal of fostering more conscious leadership worldwide. It serves as a supportive community of practice where members freely share their wisdom, tools, and experiences, elevating one another as leaders.

The Guild is more than just an organization — it's a sanctuary. It's a place where leaders can collaborate to practice and deepen their understanding of conscious leadership through love, learning, and co-creation. The Guild envisions and cultivates a world rooted in love, life, and flourishing by fostering a transformational space that balances the art of being with the necessity of doing.

Mission and Activities

The mission of the Conscious Leadership Guild is clear and urgent: to embody and ignite the call to lead with love. This mission is brought to life through a culture of open sharing, where members exchange knowledge, wisdom, and resources to help one another grow. This sharing takes many forms, including virtual gatherings, newsletters, articles, blog posts, conference calls, mentoring programs, and two annual gatherings — offered both online and in person.

One particularly meaningful initiative is the monthly virtual "Love Group." During these gatherings, members discuss their ongoing efforts to align with the Guild's purpose and mission. These meetings have been invaluable to me personally, offering insightful feedback and clear direction for implementing my next steps as a conscious leader. I am deeply grateful to my fellow Guild members for helping me test and refine some of the material in this book.

My association with the Conscious Leadership Guild has been a profound and transformative experience. It has enriched my leadership journey, provided me with a community of like-minded individuals, and reinforced my commitment to leading with love and authenticity. Through the Guild, I've witnessed firsthand the power of conscious leadership to create lasting change in the world, and I am honored to be part of this extraordinary movement.

Table of Contents

Introduction

Simple But Not Easy

Leadership wisdom integrates three elements: Head, Hunch, and Heart.

Much of the focus in organizational cultures is on developing the head, which comprises the well-known trio of data, information, and knowledge. Google search has fueled a rapid increase, which is now further accelerating through artificial intelligence. While Google has helped leaders become smarter, they aren't necessarily wiser. Leadership development programs often concentrate on skill enhancement. These factors are essential, but knowledge does not equate to knowing (which involves our heart).

Hunch encompasses foresight and intuition, resulting in insight. Hunch represents a gut feeling or an instinctive response to a particular situation. A hunch often appears as a vague sense that something is true or will occur without the clarity or confidence that typically accompanies fully formed intuitive insight.

Foresight and intuition are related concepts, yet they are not the same. Foresight entails predicting or anticipating future events through analysis and reasoning. It requires careful consideration of potential outcomes and scenarios. Although foresight can be informed by intuition and hunches, it is generally more structured and analytical, focusing on planning and preparing for what may come.

Intuition involves understanding something instinctively without conscious reasoning. Intuition often emerges from accumulated experiences, enabling individuals to make quick judgments or decisions based on a profound understanding of a situation, even if they cannot clearly articulate the reasoning. While these concepts overlap in their reliance on non-linear thinking and instinct, each serves a distinct purpose in decision-making.

While the process of wisdom development is straightforward, leaders find it difficult because the process requires that they listen to their hearts.

Heart: The Quiet Compass Within

The wisdom of our heart is not something to develop or a place to arrive at; it is a state that already resides within us. The compass we came into the world with, the inborn guide, wordlessly points us toward what is authentic, meaningful, and nourishing. Yet, as life unfolds, many leaders lose their connection to this compass. We get swept up in the expectations of others, the demands of society, and the unending quest for goals that often leave us feeling empty. Our heart's voice grows faint, buried beneath the weight of our projections and the noise of an impatient mind.

Still, our hearts are persistent. Waiting for us to return, to rediscover its clarity and wisdom. While the mind would want to control and find solutions, our heart invites trust, surrender, and flow. Our heart's wisdom is not linear nor logical but intuitive and expansive. Our heart doesn't deal in absolutes or fixed answers but offers guidance that feels whole, resonant, and deeply personal. It speaks in the language of subtle sensations and an inner knowing that cannot always be put into words. To access this wisdom, we must be willing to slow down, create space for stillness, and cultivate the resonance that lets us truly listen.

This listening is not taught. In fact, so much of what we learn growing up pulls us away from this capacity. We are taught to seek validation from outside ourselves, follow prescribed paths, and pursue the fruits of achievement at the cost of authenticity. We're encouraged to think things through, base decisions on logic and reason, and ignore the "irrational" pull of our emotions or intuition. But the wisdom of our heart cannot be accessed through intellect alone. It requires a different kind of attention — an openness, a willingness to trust in something beyond what can be measured or proven.

When we reconnect with our heart, we may discover that its wisdom often challenges the narratives we've been told about how life should be. Our heart's guidance might lead us to make decisions that defy logic or expectations. It might ask us to leave a job that looks perfect on paper but feels empty in our soul, to pursue a dream that others deem impractical, or to admit a truth we've been afraid to face. Our heart doesn't promise an easy path but offers an authentic one. When we live from it, we experience the sensation of alignment and integrity no worldly success can replace.

Heart wisdom is not just about monumental decisions; wisdom is also about minor, everyday moments. It reveals how we express ourselves and care for ourselves and others. It teaches us to let go of what no longer serves us and approach life with inquisitiveness and honesty. Our heart becomes our foundation, guiding us in the present moment and positioning us toward life in alignment with our deepest values.

But how do we learn to listen to the voice of our heart amidst the din? How do we tell the soft whispers apart from the more strident, insistent voices of fear, doubt, and ego? The answer lies in cultivating a sense of stillness within and around us. Stillness is not merely the absence of noise but an active, participatory process of tuning in and creating space for our hearts to speak. It is learning to be present with ourselves, listening without judgment, and trusting in the unfolding process.

As we practice stillness, we may begin to notice a shift. That once-elusive heart wisdom begins to turn transparent. We begin to resonate with confident choices, relationships, or paths. These moments of resonance are our heart's way of saying, "Yes, this is right for you." They may not always make sense to the mind, but they are confirmed in an undeniable way. And the more we listen, the more we learn to trust this inner compass so that it guides us with greater confidence and ease.

The journey of return to our hearts is focused inwardly, but this journey is also universal. Across cultures and traditions, our heart has been regarded as that place of wisdom and truth. Ancient teachings remind us that our heart is a physical organ and a spiritual center — a bridge between the mind and soul. Many traditions have regarded our heart as the seat of consciousness, the residence of our deepest truth. By reconnecting with this wisdom, we align with ourselves and something more significant — a sense of connection to the world around us and to the larger flow of life.

As you embark on this journey, know that our heart's wisdom is not something you need to create or earn. Our heart's wisdom is already within you, waiting to be uncovered. All this while, the compass has guided you — even when you didn't realize it. We are only asked to slow down, listen, and trust.

This journey is not about perfection; resonance is a key indicator. The journey is about learning to live from a place of authenticity, honor the truths of your heart, and trust in its wisdom even when the path ahead feels uncertain. The quiet compass within is your greatest ally, and as you learn to follow it, you will discover a life that is not just successful but meaningful, productive, fulfilling, busy, and genuinely alive. This is the wisdom of our heart, and it is here for you, now and always.

CHAPTER 1

Wisdom

"No creature can fly with just one wing. Gifted leadership occurs when heart and head — feeling and thought — meet. These are the two wings that allow a leader to soar."
— Daniel Goleman

Ancient Wisdom

As understood by ancient civilizations, wisdom was not a mere accumulation of facts or knowledge but a profound and sacred gift that patterned human lives and directed ethical conduct. Every culture added something different to the concept of wisdom, making it all the more meaningful and useful in various ways.

In ancient Egypt, the concept of wisdom was closely related to Ma'at, which symbolized truth, balance, and cosmic order. Wisdom was a reality that appeared throughout human experience, from governance and judicial system to personal conduct. Ma'at, in this view, could, therefore, be seen as empowering humans to understand and live our lives in harmony with laws at the heart of our universe. By reason and wisdom, one obtained some degree of balance and order against chaotic moments, real or figurative. Egyptian sages taught a moralistic doctrine and made one believe that real wisdom would involve an attempt toward justice, truthfulness, and morality of the soul. Furthermore, such a perception in a religious attitude points out that true wisdom has some effects on destiny in the world.

Wisdom was also valued in Mesopotamia, being accepted as one of the divine characteristics; thus, for example, the word nēmequ expresses reason or intelligence combined with spiritual knowledge. The ancient Babylonians and Assyrians regarded wise men as those who could divine the gods' will and understand the universe's complexity. Works such as the "Epic of Gilgamesh" present wisdom as a process of self-realization and ethical insight while underlining the lesson to be derived from success and failure. Wisdom gives expression to a belief in the interconnectedness of human experience and the divine, for which it was a pathway toward achieving personal and communal harmony.

The ancient Greeks advanced the concept of wisdom, which was a central theme in their philosophical discussions. In Socratic thought, wisdom entails knowing oneself and recognizing one's ignorance. Socrates asserted that a truly wise individual persistently seeks the truth through inquiry and dialogue to eliminate assumptions and foster deeper understanding. His teachings established the foundation for the philosophy of the examined life, which views the pursuit of wisdom as a moral obligation.

Plato embraced a dualistic perspective on reality, dividing existence into intelligible and sensible realms. The world of Forms (which represents the ideal, unchangeable truths that underpin the fluctuating reality we perceive) is immutable and timeless, while the physical world is subject to change and decay.

Physical entities "participate" in or "imitate" the Forms, meaning that individual objects derive their qualities from a distinction between appearance and reality and advocating for the pursuit of knowledge through philosophical reasoning.

For Plato, knowledge consists of understanding the Forms. The senses can be deceptive, whereas grasping the Forms leads to true knowledge and wisdom. Aristotle, a student of Plato, differentiated between various types of wisdom and stressed the significance of practical wisdom (phronesis) in daily life. He argued that phronesis requires the ability to deliberate on ethical actions thoughtfully, combining knowledge with experience to make well-informed decisions.

Aristotle's perspective emphasized that wisdom is not a static trait but a dynamic process requiring ongoing reflection and adaptability to life's complexities. He believed that cultivating virtues through practice is essential for achieving eudaimonia, or human flourishing, thereby more closely linking wisdom to personal fulfillment and ethical living.

In Eastern traditions, wisdom is equally significant and is often approached with a more spiritual and holistic lens. Prajñā, the Sanskrit term in Indian philosophy, refers to insight into the true nature of reality. It motivates individuals to look beyond superficial appearances to grasp deeper truths. Wisdom in Taoism advocates living in harmony with natural principles, valuing simplicity and humility in the quest for understanding.

These ancient perspectives share common themes: integrating knowledge with behavior, the importance of self-awareness, and the grace of navigating life with an appreciation for its complexities. Their insights continue shaping modern interpretations of wisdom, reminding us that true wisdom encompasses universal principles and practical application in everyday life.

Wisdom Today

Wisdom is the capacity to integrate knowledge, experience, and intuitive insights in ways that cultivate sound conclusions and ethical decision-making. It is more than the accumulation of knowledge; it is a multisensory competence that combines intellectual reasoning, emotional intelligence, and intuitive understanding. At its foundation, wisdom reflects comprehension of the complexities of leading and the awareness to act in ways that balance immediate needs with long-term consequences. Wisdom is characterized by humility, empathy, compassion, and loving. This enables leaders to consider self-limits and face challenges with clarity.

Wisdom fundamentally means discernment — the ability to see situations, relationships, and challenges for what they more deeply represent. This discernment surpasses mere comprehension to enable one to recognize patterns, anticipate consequences, and make decisions considering the bigger picture. Wise people can manage complexity, juggle multiple viewpoints, and at the same time remain self-aware. Wisdom requires intellectual humility, realizing the inherent limitations of one's knowledge, and being open to learning from others and from life itself.

Wisdom also epitomizes practical intelligence or the art of knowing when and how to apply knowledge in everyday contexts. The practical dimension weaves technical competence with emotional intelligence, ethical values, and insight into human nature to enable a person to confront difficulties with methods that balance different interests, elicit collaboration, and ensure fruitful results. Beyond finding solutions, wisdom reflects an ability to act competently.

A defining feature of wisdom is its social dimension. Our wisdom extends beyond individual capability to encompass the ability to work with diverse perspectives, mediate conflicts, and contribute to collective well-being. Wise people often inspire and empower others, sharing their insights in ways that foster growth and harmony within their communities. Their actions reflect a commitment to the highest good, often spotlighting ethical considerations and long-term benefits over instantaneous gains.

Also, wisdom embodies emotional intelligence, including empathy, self-awareness, and the possibility of self-regulation. This allows such people to feel themselves and genuinely understand other people, opening up before them and building truly trusting relationships based on consideration. Emotional intelligence enriches decision-making processes with the quality of logic and human experiences and knowledge about how those decisions may further affect other human beings.

Last but not least, intuitive insight is an essential ingredient of wisdom. Intuitive insight is the ability to resort to tacit knowledge and subconscious insights when facing uncertainty. According to Michael Polanyi, who pioneered the concept, "We know more than we can express." This is why apprenticeship and mentoring remain valuable despite formal education — some knowledge can only be conveyed through observation and practice.

Intuitive insight balances the deliberate, rational thinking that enables individuals to take action in difficult situations where a clear answer is not forthcoming. This way of knowing is beyond logic, rooted in lived experience, pattern recognition, and an alignment with more profound truths.

Ultimately, wisdom is not only a path to personal awareness and growth but also a means of fostering collective well-being. Wisdom guides people in acting with integrity and foresight, contributing to creating a more ethical and interdependent world. Wisdom is a life-long pursuit cultivated through self-reflection on our experiences and an enduring commitment to learning not just for oneself but for the benefit of others and future generations.

Wisdom Economy

The world is changing faster now than it ever has before; leaders are facing a stormy and complicated time. For many of those leaders, rapid transformation inspires anxiety rather than hope. Many leaders retreat rather than lean into the change with curiosity and openness, closing themselves to thoughts and emotions. This defensive response fosters a "me," not "we," kind of mentality, which is an essential barrier to collective progress. However, these times do require more than the transactional, self-oriented kind of leadership seen previously. We need a differently framed orientation steeped in wisdom, cooperation, and humanity.

We stand at the cusp of a different epoch as our Age of Information and Knowledge transitions to the era of wisdom. This shift ushers in what some scholars and thinkers have come to refer to as the "wisdom economy." First introduced by Earl Cook in the 1980s, the term described an economy that values experience, reflection, and insight as much as tangible resources and artificial intelligence. The wisdom economy has become a priority, reflecting another way of perceiving the world, one in which not only what we know but also how we apply that knowledge toward the greater good and sustainable development.

Information is no longer in short supply. Information is actually overwhelmingly abundant, and artificial intelligence has made access relatively simple. With the internet and other technological advances, almost anyone with a device can access more information than even the great libraries of history could have ever contained, such as the fabled Library of Alexandria. Yet, this wealth of information has not necessarily translated into greater meaning or purpose. Advanced technologies have enabled us to process and analyze data with incredible speed, affording profound insights into how the world works. As Viktor Frankl powerfully reflected in *Man's Search for Meaning*, "The greatest challenge facing humanity is the search for meaning. We have acquired incredible knowledge, yet we still struggle to live meaningful, connected lives." Reflection is the process of assimilating raw information and leveraging it for understanding. Wisdom begins when we apply the learnings from our reflections.

The wisdom economy strives to bring forth and cherish the unique gifts of every single one of us. This economy reflects a vision of society: not mere consumption but contribution. Some optimists dream of a utopian future, much as they have for earlier economic evolutions, such as moving from agrarian to industrial economies. History has also repeatedly demonstrated that steep societal changes are often accompanied by abysmal inequality and conflict. While many people live in hyper-modern cities, some residents are still trapped in outdated survivalist paradigms, the modern-day hunter-gatherers. You can see them pushing their shopping cart loaded with worldly possessions. The wisdom economy offers a different trajectory of balance, sustainability, and shared abundance.

But what distinguishes the wisdom economy from the knowledge economy that precedes it? The differences are significant and offer guidance for the future. While the knowledge economy emphasizes 'more' — more data, more efficiency, more results — the wisdom economy champions the concept of 'enough.' Wisdom urges us to pause and reflect on what we sacrifice when we gain in every area except our essential humanity. It teaches that true wealth is about having enough and achieving balance rather than relentless accumulation.

The knowledge economy values qualifications — degrees, certificates, and professional titles — as indicators of success. Although these external markers are important, the wisdom economy prioritizes empathy, compassion, and loving. In this framework, a person's character and ability to connect with others are as vital as technical skills. Job interviews in the wisdom economy evaluate candidates' knowledge and who they are: how they interact with others, face challenges, and collaborate.

Another key difference is how these economies engage with technology. The knowledge economy is fundamentally driven by technological innovation, often chasing the next breakthrough without considering long-term implications. In contrast, the wisdom economy integrates technology with human insight, applying technology thoughtfully and ethically to benefit the greater good. This approach requires balancing leaders' thoughts, emotions, and instincts to ensure that technological progress aligns with humanity's broader values and needs.

The knowledge economy emphasizes competitiveness, while the wisdom economy focuses on collaboration. The wisdom economy acknowledges that success is not a zero-sum game and that the prosperity of one individual or group is closely connected to the prosperity of others once market biases and competition are set aside. This economy reflects the understanding that we can achieve more by working together and sharing. These changes have significant implications for how business is conducted, how communities flourish, and how the world will confront its future challenges.

Another defining characteristic of the wisdom economy is reflection. While the knowledge economy celebrates innovation and speed, the wisdom economy prioritizes intentionality: reflective questioning about the purpose of actions and innovations as contributions to the common good. A reflective mindset may sometimes require slowing down, reassessing priorities, and ensuring progress does not jeopardize ethical and sustainable standards.

The shift to a wisdom economy signifies a substantial cultural transformation for workers. Knowledge workers often seek external validation through qualifications, promotions, and measurable accomplishments. In contrast, wisdom workers cultivate a more balanced perspective, focusing on their responsibilities to themselves, their communities, and the planet. They recognize that knowledge is not static or absolute; instead, experiences can be subjective and evolve along with personal growth.

The wisdom economy is also one that forces us to confront the broader consequences of our actions. Whereas it was once easy to ignore the environmental and social costs of production, distribution, and consumption, today, those costs are impossible to overlook. From climate change to economic inequality, the ripples from our choices are now evident. The wisdom economy requires circular systems that consider reuse over waste, ensuring resources are used thoughtfully and efficiently. Creativity and innovation will be at the heart of the design of such systems, imagining solutions for some of the most intractable problems facing the world.

In this emerging paradigm, listening will be more important than talking. Leaders choose to be inclusive and collaborative, focusing on sustainability, deep insight, and common sense rather than quick profits and slick presentations. Leaders must learn to combine intellectual knowledge with emotional intelligence and intuitive insight to succeed in the wisdom economy. By balancing these elements, they will find creative solutions and lead their organizations and communities with clarity and direction.

Wisdom is not something to be gained; it is inside us, only waiting to be tapped. It is about connecting with our inner resources of head, hunch, and heart and applying them to the intricacies of modern life. Those who can integrate these facets of wisdom will guide us into this new era. As we enter the wisdom economy, the solutions we seek will not be found solely in data or technology but in reflecting, connecting, and acting with intention.

Leadership Wisdom

Leadership wisdom is intricate and extends beyond mere knowledge or experience. It encompasses understanding the nuances of human behavior, making thoughtful decisions, and considering the long-term consequences of actions. A wise leader perceives reality while recognizing that individuals are interconnected within their relational contexts. Such leaders appreciate broad diversity and inclusion, fostering greater awareness and insight when navigating the complexities of their respective worlds.

Leadership wisdom signifies a deeper understanding of human nature, organizational dynamics, and the interconnectedness of decisions and consequences. Drawing from ancient wisdom traditions and modern leadership practices, it integrates practical competence with ethical discernment and emotional intelligence. Wise leaders navigate complexity while maintaining clarity of purpose and ethical integrity. They balance competing interests and make decisions that serve immediate organizational needs and broader stakeholder concerns.

Emotional intelligence at the heart of leadership wisdom makes it easier for a leader to connect with the team at a deeper level. This, in turn, builds up trust and collaboration, essential ingredients of leadership. The wise leader is sensitive not only to their own feelings but also to the feelings and needs of others. As such, the leaders make the environment so agreeable that the team members feel valued and empowered, encouraging each to give their best work.

Continuous learning and self-awareness contribute to the basis of leadership wisdom. The wise leader sustains intellectual humility while developing deep expertise in their field. They recognize patterns across different situations while remaining attuned to unique contextual factors that call for adaptive responses. Wisdom is based on experiences, yet always accessible to insight and new perspectives. Wise leaders are concerned with bringing about a culture of openness, accountability, and balance; they ensure that the actions taken will reflect the core values and principles of the organization.

Wise leaders have the ability to learn adaptively. They seek feedback and reflect on experiences of both successes and failures. The commitment to continuous learning enables them to adapt to changing circumstances and make more informed decisions in the future. Similarly, wise leaders know the value of mentoring and empowering others by investing time and effort in developing their team members. Promoting a learning and growing culture ensures that their organizations are dynamic, resilient, and capable of long-term success.

CHAPTER 2

Our Heart of Perception: Leading Through Experiences

Leaders must realize that their words, actions, and intentions will not always be interpreted as intended. A lot of international misunderstandings come from a situation that, in the sense of one party, seems OK but, from the point of view of other parties, seems very passive-aggressive or triggering. And because of this, emotional intelligence and empathy are essential leadership traits. By seeking to understand how, at least in part, the world is perceived by others, leaders will be able to close communication gaps, build trust, and establish a culture in which the need to be heard is realized. For instance, having a conversation when there are conflicts and actively listening to what others say can smoothen conflicts, strengthen hundreds of bonds in a team, etc.

Perception is a rather elaborate multistage process of sensing, organizing, and interpreting, which helps people view the world. That means being cognizant as a leader not only of one's perception but also of those within the team members, shaped by their unique experiences and inner biases. Leaders realize that perception may be subjective so that they can engage in conversations empathetically and openly. This knowledge allows them to work with diversity in thought, motive, and feeling by promoting collaboration and instituting a work culture founded on trust and mutual comprehension. Finally, a leader who exemplifies the richness of human perception will be an inspiring leader of people who understand and can direct their motives and desires effectively.

Our Heart's Influence on Leadership Perceptions

Our heart plays a deep role in shaping leadership perceptions regarding how leaders perceive others and how they are perceived in return. Thought leadership is often associated with strategy, decision-making, and intellect; research increasingly underlines the importance of emotional intelligence and empathy — those qualities are deeply tied to the "heart" — in effective leadership. The degree to which a leader can emotionally resonate with his or her team demonstrates that he or she truly cares and leads with heart, significantly impacting how he or she is perceived and interprets the needs and concerns of those being led. In many ways, our heart is foundational to the trust, motivational, and relational dimensions of leadership.

Beyond the personal level, our heart also influences how leaders frame their vision and inspire others. Leaders who communicate with emotional resonance — meaning passion about shared goals or values inspire a sense of purpose and commitment in their teams. For instance, the leader who can tell a story of why a project matters by relating it to the team's values or to a more significant societal impact will likely draw a much more robust response than one who focuses on data and metrics. This meaning shared through an emotional connection reinforces perceptions of the leader as results-driven yet purpose-driven and humane.

However, the influence of our hearts on perceptions of leadership has its complexities, too. Leaders have to balance emotional sensitivity with the requirement for objectivity and rationality. At times, very emotional responses or decisions taken wholly based on our hearts are perceived as impulsive or lacking authority. A typical example is that a leader may not want to hurt anyone's feelings and so refrains from giving constructive feedback; this inadvertently harms the growth and performance of the team. This calls for an integration of heart and head to make considered and balanced responses using emotional intelligence in a sensitive yet strategic way.

Objective Perception: A Concept of Neutral Awareness

Objective perception is to see what is without the makeup of the subjective perception. It is the endeavor to see reality in cold, disinterested terms without subjective coloring. Although absolute objectivity in perception may be impossible — since people view things from a perspective rooted in their unique experiences — the concept offers an ideal for seeing and interpreting the world accurately and without bias. It aims to remove the observer's internal filters: everything from emotions to cultural conditioning to personal experiences. For instance, if someone is practicing objective perception, they might observe a dispute between two individuals and only pay attention to the facts: what was said, how it was said, and the environment surrounding it, without developing conclusions based on their own biases or ideologies of who they think is in the "right" or "wrong." This encourages critical thinking and the intellectual maturity to detach from one's inborn bias to view circumstances or data more objectively.

Objectivity has been a philosophical debate for ages. Philosophers like René Descartes and Immanuel Kant wondered if we could ever see reality without it being filtered through our prior experiences. For instance, Kant argued that we have access to phenomena (the world as experienced) but will never experience "the things-in-themselves" (the world as it is) because our mental structures always mediate our perception. So, what I meant by objective perception was not to eliminate subjectivity but to try and minimize its impact to the most significant extent possible.

Objective perception is the essence of science and inquiry. Researchers and scientists try to observe without bias or agenda. That is why methods like double-blind studies and peer review are employed to eliminate as much bias as possible and make the observation and conclusion as objective as possible. But even in science, you cannot be 100% objective because, after all, it requires interpretation and appreciation of perspective.

In daily life, being objectively perceptive is a matter of being aware of yourself and mindful. It entails acknowledging your biases and consciously putting them aside to present the facts in a situation. In a workplace context, for instance, a leader who practices objective perception might assess someone who works for them against quantifiable results rather than whether they personally like them or not. For example, in interactions with others, someone may try to listen to others without jumping to conclusions or getting emotionally invested in how they respond, thereby making them better understand the other party's view of the situation.

Although objective perception has benefits, it also has challenges and limitations. We are sensitive, empathetic, and social beings, and our experiences, upbringing, and biases shape our responses and perceptions. Complete objectivity may, therefore, prove impossible, for even the act of observation is colored by the observer's viewpoint. But even if we cannot be completely objective, pursuing greater objectivity can help contribute to more balanced, fair, and reflective decision-making.

Fundamentally, objective perception is part of an extended set of ways to perceive and interpret the world as it is rather than the way you feel it is. While true objectivity is somewhat unattainable, it is something to aspire to. We try to become less biased and clear-headed in every situation. People can be more objective if they are mindful, self-aware, and balanced.

Subjective Perception: A Personal Lens of Reality

Subjective perception is how we see and hear what we want/expect to see/hear based on our feelings, our beliefs, what we have experienced, where we come from, cultural influences, and cognitive biases. Objective perception is more about neutrality and factual reality, showing what is happening around us. In contrast, subjective perception is something personal that depends on the person's inner world. It reflects the notion that each person's reality is different, as their thoughts, feelings, and individual history shape how they perceive and interpret the same stimulus in the outside world. Ultimately, subjective perception reminds us how deeply personal each human experience is. For instance, two individuals can stand in the same forest, surrounded by the same trees, sounds, and sights. However, one person may experience the environment as peaceful and rejuvenating, whereas the other may find it anxious or uncomfortable based on a previous challenging experience in a similar environment. This difference shows how perception gets filtered through each individual's memories, feelings, and mental associations, shaping how someone interprets the world.

Nothing is "wrong" or "flawed" with subjective perception-it's just one of the many aspects of being human. Our brains are wired to make sense of sensory information through our own experiences. The Gestalt principles of perception teach us that people tend to arrange and interpret sensory data in ways based on their mental models-which are essentially a set of beliefs and assumptions that people use to understand and navigate the world around them. When we perceive ambiguous stimuli, we frequently make inferences about what we perceive based on our expectations or beliefs, leading to perceptions that reflect our inner world as much as the outside world.

Cultural and socio-psychological factors substantially contribute to subjective perception. Traditional values, norms, and experiences condition our view of the world. For example, in some cultures, looking directly into the eyes is a form of confidence and respect; in others, it might be perceived as disrespectful. Everything, from how we perceive others to how we interpret behaviors, relationships, and even ideals such as success or happiness, gets filtered through these cultural lenses.

Emotions are another driver of subjective perception. Research in psychology has demonstrated that emotional states can profoundly affect how we interpret a given scenario. For example, a person in an upbeat mood may interpret a neutral comment as friendly or playful, whereas a person who is angry or defensive may see the same comment as negative or hostile. This emotional filtering also means that our perceptions are usually fluid, shifting with our mental and emotional state at any moment.

Subjective perception makes life interesting, diverse, and personal, but it can also lead to misunderstandings and conflicts when people fail to see that their perception is not universal. This is why effective communication and empathy go hand in hand — both focus on how individuals can dissolve the barricade between their own point of view and someone else's.

Subjective perception is a theme explored deeply in philosophy. Philosophers contend that reality is an inescapably subjective endeavor. We cannot escape our own experiences and interpretations, so we assign meaning to everything according to our perceptions. Nietzsche also stated, "There are no facts, only interpretations," meaning that all perceptions depend on the observer. Modern psychology seems to confirm this. As we previously said, we do not simply perceive reality — we create, promote, and allow it through our thoughts and experiences.

Despite its challenges, subjective perception has strengths. It creates opportunities for people to be deeply engaged with themselves, nurturing creativity, imagination, and emotional abundance. This is how art, poetry, and stories are formed through subjective perception of the world. Furthermore, subjective perception allows for empathy, our ability to connect to the feelings and experiences of others through our internal worlds. This alone is often a critical part of effective marketing campaigns.

Finally, subjective perception is an individual's personal way of seeing and understanding the outside world based on emotions, experiences, cultural aspects, and cognitive biases. Though subjective perception can sometimes cause misunderstandings or even distort the worldview, it also enriches the human experience and makes it diverse and full of meaning. So, when we realize that perception is subjective — both our own and that of others around us — we can cultivate more empathy, understanding, and connection with each other and our relationships.

Differences Between Objective and Subjective Perceptions

These are two fundamentally oppositional ways to see things. One cannot possibly pretend not to be human, that the scope of their human experience and sensations does not filter down to their perception. While perception is rooted in the external world, how one experiences that world is subjective and determined by one's internal and emotional realms, memories, cultural context, and own biases. To exemplify this difference, consider these:

For example, an objective perception in a scientific context could be taking the temperature of a room with a thermometer. As indicated by the thermometer, how hot or cold it is that day is a fact: an event in the world that is not burdened by our slant or our perspective, which anyone else using the same instrument would also see. On the other hand, subjective perception might be how different people feel at the same temperature. One person might think the room is quite cold; another, comfortably cool; and a third, slightly warm. As the thermometer's physicality remains constant, these subjective reactions are together assets like body-temperature regulation, personal experience, or preferences.

Another example is in the appreciation of art. When a group of people looks at a painting, an objective perception can describe measurable characteristics of the painting: the colors used, the dimensions of the canvas, and the techniques used by the artist. These are objective attributes that can be acknowledged regardless of opinion. Subjective perception, in contrast, occurs when individuals analyze the meaning of the painting or how it affects them emotionally. What one could see as inspiring, the other could see as sad; what one finds exhilarating, the other could find chaotic. Such interpretations say more about the people looking at the painting than the painting itself. Thus, subjectivity is not only a function of the usual way we analyze everything but also needs to be considered in light of our experiences (e.g., personal history) and feelings.

The distinction between whether a person is looking from an objective or a subjective perspective becomes even sharper in the social world. So, for example, at a workplace meeting, an objective observation might include recording facts that anyone could observe: what was said, who spoke, when the meeting started, and when it ended. While the tone of voice or body language is a rendition, it is a subjective impression. That which one person considers constructive feedback from a coworker might be another's hostile or insulting comment. The objective facts of the exchange are the same; however, these different subjective responses can be based on each person's mood, past experiences with the coworker, or even their own insecurities.

Cultural differences accentuate the divergence between objective and subjective perceptions. In some cultures, a firm handshake is seen as an assertion of confidence and respect. However, subjective understandings of that same handshake may vary significantly. Someone from a less touch-oriented culture might take the handshake as too forward or aggressive, and someone from a culture that appreciates physical proximity might find it normal or even too weak. These subjective interpretations are deeply influenced by prevailing cultural contexts and individual expectations about the nature of life, showing that the same event can mean the whole world, depending on how you look at it.

The key difference is in the emphasis: objective perceptions rest on externals, such as measurable facts independent of one's feelings or interpretation, whereas subjective perception is more deeply personal, emotion-based, and rooted in experience and culture. Knowing this may enable us to navigate human interactivity a bit more successfully when perceptions aren't aligned, and misunderstandings or conflict could occur. Understanding that the way we view the world around us may not be universal but rather just how we perceive it allows us to become more empathetic and open-minded in our relationships with others while processing and deciding in our lives.

Examples Highlighting the Difference Between Objective and Subjective Perceptions

This differentiation between objective and subjective perception takes on real-world leadership examples:

1. **Performance Evaluation:**

   Objective interpretation: A manager assessing an employee's output may look at specific numbers, such as the number of tasks performed, classes sold, or customer satisfaction ratings. These are quantifiable, observable facts that can create an unbiased judgment.

Subjective Perception: The same leader may also observe that the employee appears less enthusiastic or disengaged during meetings. While all of this could be true, it is filtered through the leader's perception of the employee's demeanor, which may stem from the leader's state of mind or preconceptions. The leader may think the employee is unengaged, but the employee may be struggling with something in their personal life outside of work.

2. **Team Conflict:**

Objective Perception: If two team members disagree, a leader who embraces objective perception may zero in on the facts of their conflict — what was said, the order in which events unfolded, or specifically, what they disagree about. This method allows the leader to gain insights into the issue without inciting partisanship.

Subjective Perception: The leader may also perceive one team member as upset or defensive. It might cause the leader to view the conflict as more personal or emotionally heated than it actually is. For instance, the leader might assume that the source of this conflict is a more profound interpersonal problem, not just a misunderstanding of what role or priority goes where.

3. **Cultural Misunderstandings:**

Objective Observation: During an international business meeting, a leader may notice that a colleague breaks eye contact immediately and speaks at a low volume. These behaviors are objective and can be observed without judgment.

Subjective Interpretation: Depending on the leader's cultural context, these behaviors can be interpreted as disinterest or lack of confidence. However, in the colleague's culture, these behaviors may be respectful or, at the very least, professional. Without knowing the cultural context, the leader's subjective perception may lead to inaccurate assumptions about the colleague's intention or ability.

4. **Feedback Delivery:**

Objective perception: A leader giving feedback may observe the specific behaviors or outcomes, such as missed deadlines or errors in a report, and deliver remarks in clear, factual terms.

Subjective Presentation: The perception of tone (or the way it is presented) can vary with the emotional state of the employee receiving the feedback. If they feel insecure, for example, they may read the feedback as overly critical, even if the leader's intention was constructive.

CHAPTER 3

The Inseparable Dance of Wisdom and Heart

"The shortest course in Wisdom is never about ideas and practices. It is about traversing those twelve inches between the head and our heart."

The Wisdom Way of Knowing.
Cynthia Bourgeault (2003)

Speaking of wisdom and heart as parallel entities is missing the point. The threads interweave into the essence that defines a human being. Neither really could exist without the other; they are the sides of one coin, with the true value revealing itself through the other. In its total manifestation, our heart is about empathy and compassion, leading to unconditional loving.

True wisdom is not merely a collection of knowledge but a realization of how things are interconnected. In other words, our actions influence not only what is within our sphere but also the broader web of life. It fosters empathy and a profound understanding of our shared humanity. From empathy and compassion, loving naturally blossoms, guiding our actions and decisions.

Loving is acting out this bonding: acknowledging the other as worthy and dignified, a devotion to the good of the other beyond the limitations of the self. However, loving unreflectively is trying to navigate a ship without a rudder at the mercy of erratic currents of feelings. It can easily run off course, even become destructive, bereft of the clarity of vision that wisdom would provide.

Aware, erudite — even bursting with quotations from every philosophical text and convoluted theory apart from the guiding force of loving — a person can be inhumane in action and speak without warmth. Though big and grand, it stays sterile, knowledge that cannot be fulfilled. It is the danger of wisdom without loving.

When wisdom and loving are combined, allowing them to dance in harmonious balance, their true power is unleashed. Tempered by compassion and caring, wisdom leads our actions to deep understanding. Loving, illuminated by the discerning light of wisdom, calls forth a ray of hope that can empower us to create bridges connecting toward a world for the highest benefit of all concerned.

The dance of wisdom and loving is not some form of passivity but an ongoing active pursuit. It invites us into self-awareness, plumbing the depths of our hearts and minds to confront our biases and challenge our notions. It summons empathy, the practice whereby one stands outside of one's experiences and truly sees and understands the world through other eyes.

Further exploring the interplay of wisdom and loving reveals the intricacies of the human experience, woven together by the unique strands that each of us contributes to the fabric of life. Such complexity presents us not as islands but as threads in an elaborate tapestry, each action resonating like a note in a symphonic score, rippling out to unbind us from the self-centered notion of a solitary existence. Our relationships act as the dew dripping that nurtures our growth and inspires us to challenge the limits of egotism.

Wisdom is not merely something to believe in; it is something to live by, as wisdom is always more than just knowledge. This awareness encourages us to consider not only our goals but also their consequences. It is that quiet suggestion to act with consciousness, each of us creating waves that touch others, our still water rippling outward. Wisdom, in this sense, serves as a mirror that enables us to see the interwoven threads of our collective humanity and compassion, inspiring us to tread lightly upon the earth.

On the other hand, when expressed fully, loving sparks divine inspiration that drives us forward. However, it must be grounded in the reality reflected by the lens of wisdom. Without this balance, our loving can become an all-consuming wildfire, sweeping away everything in its wake, blind to the more significant consequences. This is where we need to be discerning, admitting that loving is not a willful blindness but an active embrace of the web of intricacies beyond us.

The union of these two forces creates a powerful synergy that enables growth and understanding. This partnership calls on us to have dialogues that disrupt our points of view, listen with intention, and act with intention. It summons a dedication to valuing those things that bring us together, embracing our diversities as we strive for archaeological commonality.

Wisdom and loving dance together, and everything dynamic influences the world around us. This is a demand in the name of action, urging us to break the drought of inaction and engage thoughtfully with the Politics of Dystopia. This leads each of us on a path where every step we make can either raise or lower the spirit of all humanity.

As we navigate this process, we must stay true to ourselves and find balance and peace in the journey that transforms us. There, wisdom and loving join together as one, forming a flickering light of hope to guide the way. Our lives are not simply our own; they dance within the lives of others.

Digging deeper, the dance between sage and lover is at the core of who we are. It is a rhythm of whispers in which we all play a part in this grander symphony called life. In this complex tapestry, we exist not as mere individuals but as pieces of a more elaborate puzzle, where every engagement resonates through infinity. The richness of our relations, which extend beyond the concern of self-interest, makes our development come alive.

Wisdom hones consciousness that is so much more than the amassing of knowledge. It shrouds light, illuminating every choice. This light invites us not just to glance at intent but to gaze into effect. It is a gentle reminder of how our individual actions have the power to send ripples that reverberate through the lives of others. In that way, wisdom reflects the deep complexity of how we share the world together, reminding us to tread gently on this earth.

In the intersection of these two forces lies a unique synergy encouraging growth and understanding. This partnership requires conversations that challenge our perspectives, the desire to hear, and intentional action. It is a challenge to make sure we nurture the bonds of the community, celebrate what sets us apart, and seek out the ground we share.

And so now, the dynamic force of this dance of wisdom and loving is in motion in our interactions with the world. It is a summons to stand against apathy and engage thoughtfully in the plethora of strife that surrounds us. On this journey, each step either aids or injures the common human spirit.

On this never-ending journey, may we strive to keep that balance where transformation will be unleashed. This is wisdom, yet is loving, and is a radiant star shining bright that illuminates the path. For lives are not simply ours; they are enmeshed with those of others, and each moment is a choice to feel for the greater good, to tell the story of compassion that goes beyond ourselves.

CHAPTER 4

Guidance from Our Heart

Our Heart's Wisdom: A Compass for Authentic Living and Leadership

We hear things like follow and listen to our heart, but what does that mean for us? Are they idle sentimental notions to get us to give in to momentary pleasures or act spontaneously? Far from it. Print and radio were words, music, and sounds, moving through the air as a breath through a mouth — the wisdom of our heart is profound, intuitive, and grounded in the courage of being. It does not push us to deliberation or excess but hints to us as to what is real, what is worth attention, and what goes with the essence of our true self. Our heart is not the enemy of reason but its companion, with a deeper, more holistic sense of life's complexities. It balances the mind's reasoning with an instant knowing that moves beyond facts and figures, steering us to choices that align with our more human selves.

What's remarkable about our heart's wisdom is that it is the bridge between thought and feeling, a balance of reason and emotion that brings us to our most authentic selves. Its message is not to forsake reason and logic but to broaden our understanding by recognizing the finer, lesser-noticed aspects of our experience. The mind is great for logic but never for wisdom; let it go — our heart knows what we need to hear: true voice, true loving, true us. And that gives us the ability to live and lead according to our values, making decisions that are not only wise but also soulful, fulfilling, and ethical.

The Modern Disconnect from Our Heart

But in today's world — especially in leadership — heart wisdom is generally treated as foolish or irrelevant. We inhabit a culture of intelligence worship, where logic, analysis of data points, and results on a ledger are adjudicated as god and ideology. We are conditioned early in life to favor the mind, to be rewarded for trendy mantras in the world and outward thinking rather than be validated from within. In the workplace, this bias translates into decision-making processes prioritizing data, metrics, and "hard facts" over intuition, emotion, and human connection.

This is especially true of leaders, who are often under extraordinary pressure to achieve quantifiable, immediate results. "People don't act according to their heart in this world," a client said of such environments, where our heart's quiet wisdom can seem either out of place or counterproductive. A leader discussing intuition or emotional resonance runs the risk of being written off as "soft" or unprofessional. But this disconnection from our hearts has a price to pay. The mind can solve a myriad of technical problems at once and analyze nearly infinite streams of data but is sometimes not equipped to perceive larger realities or larger dynamics. The intellect counts the pieces; our heart sees the whole. It senses the thread that binds people, relationships, and purpose, applying deep yet meaningful insights.

To take one specific example, a leader faced with a decision to restructure their team. Of course, the mind will obsess over efficiency metrics, productivity reports, and budget constraints to come up with a solution that seems perfect on paper. Our heart, however, may feel the cost of such moves, knowing the importance of trust, morale, and even cohesion, which may not easily be documented and is essential for future success. Disregarding our heart's wisdom in such instances risks a solution being technically solid yet fundamentally unsustainable.

The Science Behind Our Heart's Wisdom

Modern research is starting to confirm what some spiritual traditions have suspected for ages: that our heart is much more than a mechanical life-sustaining pump. It is integrally involved in when and how we feel emotions, understand events, and perceive our surroundings. Recent discoveries in neurocardiology show that our heart has a nervous system of its own — a "heart-brain" that sends continuous messages to and from the brain in our heads. This is not a one-way street of communication. Signals from our heart modify the brain, controlling emotional regulation, cognitive clarity, and even decision-making, establishing a feedback organism that shapes the way we feel, think, and act.

Perhaps the most interesting initial finding to come out of this research is the discovery of our heart's electromagnetic field, which may be the largest and most potent electromagnetic field produced by the human body. The preliminary research indicates that this field goes out a few feet beyond the body and interacts with the environment, affecting the emotional state of anyone nearby. Research shows that when we are coherent emotionally — calm and compassionate, and our head and heart are in sync — this field settles down and opens up, and we are filled with connection to and trust in other people. On the contrary, when we are stressed, anxious, and lack internal connection, the field becomes electric and creates tension and discomfort.

This understanding has significant implications for leaders. It implies that the leader's emotional condition can, in turn, impact the emotional state of their team or organization. When leaders are centered, calm, and aligned with the wisdom in their hearts, they create an environment of trust, collaboration, and positivity. However, if a leader's heart is absent — calculating purely based on metrics and outcomes — they may, even though they mean well, inadvertently create stress, disengagement, or mistrust.

Our Heart's Intuitive Wisdom

When we deeply engage with these teachings, we realize that our heart is intuitive in ways that are difficult to put into words and that the findings turn out to be scientific insights beyond the head. It senses truths that the analytical mind is unable to perceive, leading us not via facts and logic but by feelings of resonance, gentle nudges, and an internal sensation of "rightness." This information is rooted not in random or rash decisions; it comes from a place of deep alignment with our values, our experiences, and the web of life.

Reflect on times in your life when you had an unexplainable pull toward a choice, person, or path. Maybe you sought a career that didn't make sense to others but that you felt deep in your heart was the sacred path. Or perhaps you just knew that a certain relationship wasn't right, even when every other detail looked perfect on the outside. This clarity arises from our soul or who we authentically are

— it cuts through the clamor of what could be alleged failures or follies to highlight what is, at its core, important.

For leaders, this kind of intuitive wisdom is priceless. It enables them to withstand uncertainty confidently, make choices that reflect their principles, and relate to others on a higher, more authentic level. For instance, a leader could have a gut feeling that a team member is in distress even if they are not externally showing signs of struggle. Following this intuition — offering a listening ear, compassion, and resources — builds trust and makes people feel a sense of belonging that radiates through teams and improves the organization.

Overcoming the Fear of Listening to Our Heart

Though it is deeply wise, trusting our hearts can seem dangerous — especially in a society that values the logic and certainty of the head. Many leaders balk at leaning into their instincts, worried they will make a poor choice, be critiqued for their decisions, or be led by emotion. These fears are valid but come from how deeply we have been taught to distrust our instincts. Reawakening the wisdom of our hearts means unlearning these patterns and learning a new relationship with ourselves — honoring intuition is as vital as honoring intellect.

One of the greatest challenges is separating the voice of our heart from the louder, more insistent voices of fear, ego, or impulse. Fear tends to issue immediate commands or threats requiring action or retreat; our heart whispers gently, offering calm, steady guidance. Ego craves praise and acknowledgment, leading us toward decisions that will gain the approval of the outside world — decisions that make us appear good but don't land in our true being. Our heart, by comparison, leads us to a place of harmonious being and feeling, and even when it guides us onto a difficult or uncharted path, we feel aligned with our best selves.

It takes practice to learn discernment. It asks us to slow down, make room for contemplation, and listen inward. Things like meditation, journaling, or spending time in nature allow us to quiet the mind and connect with what our heart knows. Gradually, we come to recognize that the voice of our heart arises as a feeling of expansion, clarity, and authenticity — an inner "yes" that feels true, even when it doesn't make sense or match the external world.

The Courage to Follow Our Heart

Our heart is not socially palatable; it takes courage to listen deeply since its wisdom may not be what external circumstances or the world expects to read on their screen. It might encourage us to take the leap, to embrace the unknown, or to surrender that which no longer serves us, however safe or familiar it might be. For instance, our heart may urge us to resign from a stable but uninspired job, chase a dream that others would consider unrealistic, or leave an intimate relationship that's lost its authenticity. Such choices can be challenging because they usually call us to face fear, the unknown, and the judgment of others. But our heart's wisdom also offers the prospects of profound liberation, tapping us into a life that expresses who we are — not who we think we should be.

Decisions that come from our hearts often result in deeply satisfying experiences, even when they don't add up in the beginning. One sample strategy could be a leader with an ear to the ground who might put people before profits, forging a relationship of trust between the company and team, which ultimately yields better results. Likewise, a person who listens to their heart when it comes to a personal choice — like pursuing a creative calling or leaving a toxic relationship — may experience short-term discomfort but will ultimately be better aligned and joyful.

The Relational Wisdom of Our Heart

The wisdom of our heart is not just proprietary; it is deeply relational. When we lead from our heart, we treat others with more kindness, empathy, and authenticity. Our senses sharpen to the needs and emotions of the people around us, and space to feel authentic connections opens up. In a leadership scenario, this translates into building trust, a sense of collaboration, and a shared vision. Our heart knows that strength isn't about power or dominion; it's about vulnerability and receptivity. It also means that by being true to ourselves, we can serve others and foster relationships based on understanding and respect.

We are the ones who create the waves. By living authentically and kindly, we encourage others to follow suit, fostering a community of connection, compassion, and shared humanity.

Practicing Heart-Led Leadership

As we contemplate our heart in the context of our own life and leadership, how often do we actually take the time to listen to it? How many of our decisions happen because what we sense to be true trumps what makes sense or what we expect? What will change in our lives if we stop listening to our minds and listen to the whispers of our hearts?

The voice of our heart is not a path that is linear; it is a practice that deepens over time as we learn how to listen to our silent navigation system inside. It urges us to join together our mind and our heart, logic, and intuition so that we may meet the complexities of life with grace and integrity. And the answers we look for are not out there; the answers are here, waiting for us to find them. By listening to our hearts, we begin to live and lead in a fuller, richer way that recognizes what we do and who we are.

CHAPTER 5

Silence Speaks

"Let Silence speak to you about the secrets of the universe."
— Rumi

Our Heart's Wisdom: Listening to What Matters in Stillness

Heart wisdom is typically revealed in silence. When nothing demands our attention and the relentless chatter of the mind quiets down, our heart speaks — quietly but no less powerfully, in its rightful place. Its direction does not scream, shout, or compete with the mind's loud, desperate voice. Instead, it patiently sits in the silence, offering wisdom and clarity for those willing to slow down long enough to hear. But in a society that glorifies busyness and constant productivity, we shriek at silence, avoid it, and even fear it. To embrace stillness, to deliberately lean into the quiet, is often countercultural and, at some points, profoundly uncomfortable.

Stillness is an invitation to meet ourselves at the core of who we are — not who we project to be, not how the world sees us, but who we are at the essence of our being. It removes the facades we build, the characters we inhabit, and the distractions we cling to in order not to see beneath this thin layer of visibility. But how frequently do we run from this meeting? We occupy each spare moment with noise and stimuli, so we have no time to spare to look back at ourselves, which leaves us chasing away the fear of silence. We grab our phones at the slightest hint of boredom, switch on the television to ease the silence of a vacant room, or throw ourselves into an endless to-do list to keep the mind engaged and our heart's whispers at bay. In the modern world, it has become so easy — almost automatic — to avoid silence; in doing so, we inadvertently cut ourselves off from this depth of understanding.

But why does silence feel so threatening? For many, the issue is the mind's response to stillness. As soon as we allow ourselves to sit in silence, our mind starts flushing away the silence with fear, doubt, judgments, and the all-time to-do lists that sound like music. Our ego (the part of us that craves certainty and control) doesn't like silence because it thrives on action and distraction. It fears stillness, where nothing is under its dominion. But when we create room for stillness, something deeper, more contemplative, starts to surface. We have to go below the noise of the mind to access our heart and the wisdom therein, which is elusive as long as we are caught up in frenetic activity.

Our Heart's Gentle Voice

The voice of our heart is entirely different from the voice of the ego. Where the ego shouts in absolutes, urgency, and fear, our heart whispers in gentler, quieter tones. It does not require or demand; instead, it provides, resonates, and harmonizes and, at the most basic level, provides peace or clarity. Our heart guides us to what feels genuine, accurate, and authentic. But in order to heed the voice of our heart, we must develop presence, silence, and patience. We need to be ready to sit with the discomfort of the unknown, to embrace silence not as the void but as an open space of chance — a chasm of potential.

To listen to the voice of our heart, you need faith — the desire to relinquish the mind's sense of certainty and control. It asks us to lean into the quiet, to let the stillness expand without hurrying to fill or define it. This can be hard, especially in a culture that values speedy answers and rapid results. But the wisdom of our heart does not run on the mind's schedule. It gives direction in the language of time, the music of the stars, and whispers that the mind is unable to hear.

Silence as a Portal into Heart-Opening Wisdom

Silence is not void; it is filled with meaning; it lives and breathes. We can hear the whispers of our heart in silence, the things that are unspoken but need to be heard often in the hustle and bustle of life. When we allow ourselves to pause, to enter into the hush, we start to become aware of what we genuinely feel, what we require, and what we might have been evading. This is what makes silence so uncomfortable — it forces us to face who we are. But only through such encounters can we access the wisdom of our heart and find a way to live that is more aligned with our truth.

Making stillness in a world that valorizes busyness can feel like a radical act, but it is also critically needed. Stillness is not the same as giving up on life or running away from its difficulties. In fact, stillness allows us to reconnect with what defines us at our core. It helps us unhook ourselves from the clamor, the distractions, and the pull of the world, creating space for our heart's soft whisper to emerge.

Meditation is the Act of Listening

Meditation is one of the most powerful practices for cultivating stillness. It creates a space where attention can be given to everything at once, a moment to observe our thoughts without attaching any judgments or nonjudgments. Meditation is not about "stopping" our thoughts, as it is popularly perceived; instead, it is about creating spaciousness to witness them without attachment, preventing our thoughts from overwhelming us. Here, we start to notice the difference between the mind's chattering and our heart's deeper, still voice.

To start, dedicate five minutes to your breath. Notice your chest rise and fall with the breath. Feel the breath entering and leaving your body. And when, not if, the mind drifts-notice and gently return to the breath. The mind will resist at first, raising thoughts of doubt, agitation, or fear. This is natural. It's about staying present, breathing into whatever discomfort may be, and trusting that beneath the surface cacophony, our heart waits to be heard. As the practice becomes deeper over time, you will start to awaken to moments of stillness even while the mind is running. Within this spaciousness, the whispers of our heart become more discernible.

Contemplation: Constant and Intentional Reflection

Contemplation, the practice of deep, deliberate reflection, is a different means of stillness. In contrast to goal-oriented problem-solving, contemplation is not about reaching conclusions or solutions. It's about sitting with a question, an idea, or an experience and letting it unfold organically without judgment or control. Contemplation is an invitation to enter the inner world with openness and curiosity, shaping an environment within which the wisdom of our hearts may emerge.

For instance, one could walk in nature and ponder something that's been troubling them, not with the goal of solving it but to see what comes up. One might sit with a piece of music, artwork, or even a moment of beauty in silence as they allow it to resonate within them. They give themselves the space to feel their responses without immediately moving toward interpretation or analysis. In these quiet moments of reflection, the mind quiets, and the insights of our hearts start to bubble up.

Nature: A Mirror of Stillness

Indeed, nature may be one of the most familiar and deep-rooted partners in recognizing stillness. When we enter nature, we are reminded of rhythms and cycles that occur outside the chaos of human life. The wind in the trees, the rush of a river, and the infinite sky above all request that we pause, breathe, and be. Nature provides us with a mirror of the inner peace we search for.

A walk in the woods, time spent before the ocean, or even a few minutes in a garden can provide the space for our heart's voice to emerge. These moments are not only sacred to ourselves but also to something more — something bigger than ourselves, more eternal and transcendent.

Small Moments of Pause

Stillness needn't involve endless meditation or retreating into the void. Instead, it can be sprinkled as small, intentional breaks throughout daily life. For example, pause for a second before responding to an email, close your eyes and take a few deep breaths, or spend five minutes before a meeting walking outside and feeling the sun on your face. Even three minutes of deep, conscious breathing can provide a burst of calm amid a busy day.

Those little interventions of presence pull us back into this moment, the abode of our hearts. They show us in subtle ways that stillness isn't something we find when we stop moving, but when we move, it might be done with awareness, intention, and a desire to listen.

The Voice of Our Heart

When we carve out this space for stillness, our hearts' wisdom often emerges in surprising ways. It might feel like sudden clarity about a decision we've been grappling with, a feeling of peace that envelops us, or an intuitive nudge that leads us to our next steps. Our heart wants no heroic gestures or theatrical revelations; it is not a speech-maker but only a whisper, a low murmur sounding only to those who will listen.

When we begin to experiment with the practice of stillness in our lives, we may be surprised to find that the voice of our heart is nothing like we expected. It is not loud or insistent. It doesn't holler or try to talk over you. It's calm, steady, and deeply resonant. The better we listen, the more we hear it as the truest expression of who we are.

Silence is not an escape from life; it is a return. The world and its chatter fade within silence, and we are left with the simplicity of the now. In such simplicity, our heart speaks — not our heart that uses words, but our heart that uses a language we understand instinctively. Its wisdom is ever-present, just waiting for us to stop, breathe, and hear.

So listen: What might we hear if we permitted ourselves to be still? What truths would come to light if we listened to our hearts? Our heart has its wisdom. Our heart is always speaking. We just have to listen. In the silence, in the stillness, perhaps we can finally hear the clarity, the peace, and the truths we needed to hear all along.

CHAPTER 6

The Courage to Feel

"It was not time that healed; it was your courage to feel everything you used to run away from. Being with yourself and meeting your tension is hard, but it is the only way to release everything that has been bottled up inside of you. Your pain was simply asking for your attention."

— yung pueblo

Emotional Intelligence

Leaders attending EI courses but deciding not to feel — reveal a chasm between understanding with the mind and choosing to embody that learning. It is about building self-awareness, empathy, and emotional management as the foundation for how we make decisions and work with others, rather than just how we read books and theories. Daniel Goleman, one of the early proponents of emotional intelligence, said that EI is not just about knowing how to relate well to people but also involves leaders dovetailing well with their emotions and using that approach to influence their behaviors and interactions with people. Yet, if leaders relate to EI as a menu of skills rather than as a transformational way of life, they know the concepts cognitively but do not fully translate the content into their lived experience. One reason leaders may opt not to feel, despite EI training, is that emotional engagement requires vulnerability — a characteristic many leaders perceive as a liability in high-stakes environments.

In her research on vulnerability and leadership, Brené Brown argues that being open to one's emotions necessitates confronting uncertainty, risk, and emotional exposure, which can be uncomfortable—especially for those who project control and authority. Leaders often fear that this openness might undermine their perceived strength or competence, leading them to suppress their feelings instead of engaging with them. This avoidance impedes personal development since taking risks is vital for growth, and it ultimately harms relationships within their teams.

This is not an isolated issue — organizational cultures influence each leader's work. As a result, the belief that emotions are inappropriate to display at work and detract from work success is pervasive and still considered the socially acceptable approach to dealing with emotions in many workplaces. Goleman and Boyatzis theoretically argue that because organizations rarely create an environment that normalizes or encourages emotional engagement, leaders see a pragmatic impulse toward emotional detachment as the prudent and acceptable way forward.

No matter how much training they receive in EI, if their working environment fails to reflect emotional valence, they may lack opportunities to practice and integrate these procedures into their everyday work lives. In addition, some leaders may not have yet developed the emotional self-awareness needed to engage with their feelings fully. Emotional intelligence begins with acknowledging and naming one's feelings, yet many people have been trained to deny or avoid their feelings altogether.

Neuroscience research by Richard Davidson has shown that emotional suppression can develop into a habitual response, hindering the individual's ability to feel. While EI courses can help raise awareness, they do not tend to provide ongoing support or practice opportunities to facilitate the disbandment of these deeply embedded habits; leaders can become intellectually aware without being moved to action.

Expressive and emotional learning is needed in EI courses, particularly if we are to fill this gap between whether EI is being taught, how it is being taught, and when it is being taught. Leaders must be inspired to truly feel and express their emotions in a safe and caring sphere. Organizations must cultivate cultures that value and represent emotional engagement, showing that EI is more than individual skill; it is a collective vow towards authenticity and relationship building.

Heart and Emotions

Our heart is not just a source of wisdom; it is also a place where our deepest feelings take root. It is the home of all things raw and real about our human experience. Yet, even with their central role in life, emotions are often misunderstood, feared, or even dismissed. Society teaches us to control our feelings, to hide them, or to "get over them" as fast as possible so we can return to being functional, productive, and composed. But this comes at a cost. Our heart's wisdom doesn't emerge when we shut the door on our emotions.

To feel is to step into the fullness of life, yet this act of courage is often met with resistance. We live in a world that rewards stoicism and celebrates distractions. The discomfort of sadness, the vulnerability of love, and the burning intensity of anger are emotions we are taught to manage, control, or even ignore. By numbing the pain, we also numb connections and insights of truths that emotions carry. To feel is to open the door to our own humanity and to a deeper understanding of what it means to be alive.

To feel deeply engages with the fullness of life in all its beauty and complexity. But to feel deeply also requires courage. This is a radical kind of courage in a culture that so often equates vulnerability with weakness. It asks us to give up the idea of emotions as a problem that needs resolution and instead accept them as central, powerful, and vital aspects of ourselves.

The Messages of Emotions

Every emotion we feel carries meaning, a message, and a profound truth about our inner world.

Grief, for example, is not just pain of loss but evidence of love. It indicates how much one was attached to someone or something dear. We learn about impermanence, about how precious our bonds are, about how resilient the human spirit is through grief. Grief allows us to recall the past, celebrate it, and grapple with how, even though we may have lost what we loved a long time ago, pieces of it are still a part of us. To grieve is not to be weak; it is to remember, to seed in our souls what we had so that knowing this, we may someday flower once more with all the richness of such memories.

Likewise, anger is not just heat or tension — it's a signal, a guide. It's triggered when something we care about is about to be taken from us or when we detect injustice. When acknowledged and interpreted, anger, often dismissed as corrosive, becomes a clarion call for action. It calls on us to protect our boundaries, to speak up about what's right and wrong, or to fight for what we care about. Channeling anger into positive change can motivate us to advocate for ourselves and others and turn frustration into progress.

Fear, in contrast, illuminates our vulnerabilities and the tender places within us where trust falters. It asks us to identify what we fear losing or having to confront and dares us to uncover whether the conflict is a real or imagined threat. Fear, when embraced, is the teacher of courage. It encourages us to enter the unknown, develop resilience, and fortify our trust in ourselves and our faith in the world around us.

The data in this are complex, but joy, however sweet and transient, is no less so. It has moments of levity and beauty, but it also demands our openness to its transience. To fully take on joy is to acknowledge that it is fleeting and can sweep in and out as quickly as a wave. Yet, doing so finds us invited to be fully here — relishing the sweetness of the now without gripping at it. Joy teaches us to be grateful for life as it comes to us, to appreciate the transient and small, and to value the beauty of life itself.

Love, the most fragile and transformative of emotions, invites us to risk it all. When we love deeply, we risk loss, rejection, or heartbreak. But love is what connects us to something larger than ourselves — our shared humanity, our sense of belonging, and our essence. Love is beyond our individual wit, creating a web of shared experiences of giving or receiving. It's the gravity that pulls us to greater heights and shows us what it means to be human: imperfect, least of all perfect, and indefatigably connected.

Every single one of these emotions — and all the rest we experience — are messengers with wisdom to offer. They are not random, senseless acts — rather, they are signs showing us where to grow to become more self-aware. But when we try to suppress or ignore these emotional signals, we cast aside some of their deepest lessons. When we suppress an emotion, it doesn't just disappear; instead, it lingers in our systems, showing up in the form of tension, anxiety, or behaviors that no longer serve us. To ignore them is to silence a whisper that becomes a scream in time. Our heart knows this — it knows that healing doesn't start by fleeing from our feelings but by leaning into them with curiosity and compassion.

Building emotional courage is the ability to feel, allow, and honor our feelings without fear or judgment. It doesn't mean allowing our feelings to drive the bus or dwelling in them forever. Instead, emotional courage calls us to allow our feelings room to be felt and unpacked. Emotions are waves — they rise, they crest, and they fall. If we let ourselves sit with them, they teach us what we need to know, and then they set us free to leave behind the past with more clarity, strength, and understanding.

Tools for Emotional Courage

When we have avoided or suppressed our emotions for most of our lives, they may feel very oppressive at times. For many, releasing these feelings may invoke a sense of vulnerability: will they be too hard to handle? The emotions feel overwhelming only if we don't attempt to feel them. If we show up for them with space and compassion, they start to melt into softening, giving us their gems of wisdom and helping us walk through them more easily. And the wonderful thing is that there are tools and practices that can help you do just that, with self-awareness, self-empathy, self-compassion, and self-loving.

They can be transformed into something that will help us grow and heal rather than fearing and self-judging.

Perhaps journaling is among the simplest ways to connect with our feelings. Writing out thoughts and feelings is also an immensely powerful process of what is going on inside of us. Quite often, when we are processing in our heads, emotions can be vague or messy pit stains in our brains, and verbalizing them makes them real, less abstract. It also provides a safe space without judgment to explore our internal world, free to discover what it sounds or looks like without concern for how it would sound or look to others. We can begin, for example, with simple but profound questions like: What am I feeling now? Was there a stirred emotion? Exactly which one was it? What is this feeling trying to tell me? That way, it makes sense to you, first and foremost, before you ever reveal what's within you. It allows us to know and relate more to ourselves so we may look inside of ourselves with curiosity, not agony.

Another essential practice for working with emotions is somatic awareness, or how our body relates to our feelings. Emotions do not exist only in the mind — they manifest as bodily sensations. Grief might weigh in our chest, anger can manifest as tightness in our jaw or fists, and anxiety might cause our stomach to clench. Such emotions can be stored in the body and released through movement through yoga or even gentler breathwork to help the movement of those emotions move through us fully. We don't need to make this process more complicated: simply placing a hand over our heart, closing our eyes, and breathing slow, deep breaths are enough to create a sense of safety and calm inside our body that then affirms that it is safe to feel whatever arises.

For those wishing to have a more interior and less loud mode, there stands the very real prospect of meditation. During meditation, we concentrate on our breath. We feel the emotions without being overwhelmed by them. Endure being with emotions; do not go into them, get swept up in them, feed them; do not try to make them go away. Most importantly, as we begin to feel, acknowledge our feelings as they come present, name them, do so without judgment, and remember that whatever that feeling is, even if it is profound, it will not last forever. This is all about cultivating inner stability while our feelings may feel rocky.

At the same time, creative expression might also form that connection, allowing one to tap into and enter some deep-seated areas inside our bodies that may elude us but will definitely touch areas the words aren't quite touching. Arts, music, and other expressions help process instincts through therapeutic outlets. We allow our emotions an outlet for flow-through via the medium of painting, song, and movement; energy that would perhaps otherwise become pain is dissipated, and the pains of life can manifest in beauty. We don't need to be artists or performers to benefit from this creative expression; it's about creating. Draw, write verses, and dance around the living room. It can be cathartic to create something from our feelings, any creation, really, as a way to spin them into something to hold.

As a last note, remember that emotional courage has nothing to do with trying to do it all ourselves. And often, what we do best is the endeavor of reaching out to the presence of others. Whether it be a trusted friend we confide in, a support group we join, or even a coach or therapist we see, talking to people about how we feel is so freeing. Talking our feelings through with another human being builds connection and gives us the knowing that we are not battling alone.

Support doesn't always need to be solution-based; sometimes, feeling heard and validated is enough to lighten the emotional load we carry. Asking for support does not denote weakness — it is a courageous exercise in self-care and self-love.

These tools — journaling, somatic practices, meditation, creative expression, and seeking support — are not about "fixing" our emotions or making them go away. Instead, they invite our emotions to be, feel, and move through us on their own time. Each practice allows us to create a safe, intentional, and compassion-filled environment to connect, experience, and sit with our emotions. Through this process, we will realize a deeper relationship with our inner world, wherein the gift to transform a hurricane of emotion into a compass for healing and self-exploration is forged.

Sitting with Discomfort

Perhaps one of the biggest challenges of emotional courage is learning to sit with discomfort. When sadness comes crashing over us, when anger rises up, or fear tightens its grip on us, the instinct very often is to run away — to distract, to numb the pain, to shove those emotions out of sight. But discomfort is not a thing to be afraid of; it is part of being human. Sitting in discomfort is recognizing our feelings but avoiding attempting to remedy or alter them. It's saying, "I see you. I hear you. I am here with you."

Discomfort is not permanent. It's like any emotion in life, which ebbs or flows, comes or goes. When we let ourselves be present with it, we may begin to notice it soften and see what is real beneath. Maybe our sadness says we are capable of love, our anger wants us to take action, and our fear urges us to trust ourselves even more.

Honoring Our Feelings

To honor our feelings is to honor ourselves. It is OK that every emotional reaction we have is valid, no matter how inconvenient, messy, or challenging to confront. Honoring our feelings doesn't mean being ruled by our feelings but giving them space without judgment. It means allowing ourselves to cry, laugh, rest, rage, and celebrate. It is trusting that our heart can absorb it all.

Knowing through our heart is a piece of wisdom that comes from feeling at the deepest level and being free. Our feelings are much more than mere disturbances of our inner peace: allowing them to exist opens the door to healing, growth, and deeper self-knowledge. It is not the absence of hurt or unending bliss but simply being fully alive to complexity and wholeness.

In the experience of feeling deeply, we truly live. Through that fullness of life, we discover our heart's infinite power, resilience, and grace.

CHAPTER 7

Aspects of Our Heart – Self-Empathy, Self-Compassion and Self-Loving

Self-Empathy versus Self-Awareness

Are self-awareness and self-empathy the same? While they both serve the context of personal development, they have varying purposes and relevant mental implication processes.

Self-awareness is the capacity to recognize and comprehend our own thoughts, feelings, and behaviors, and this relates to recognizing the outside experience of each person. In other words, we are aware and able to articulate how we feel/think and act over time. This skill illuminates valuable insights and perspectives for life choices when adequately utilized in personal development.

Self-empathy involves caring concerns and understanding thoughts, feelings, and experiences. More than just recognition, it's an action of nurturance toward an inner, kind, and supportive dialogue. Treating ourselves with the same kindness and care we would offer a close colleague who is struggling is what self-empathy is all about. This may include allowing ourselves to feel our emotions and, when things happen that we label bad, being understanding and patient with our weaknesses and mistakes.

While self-awareness lets us know what we are experiencing, self-empathy shows how to treat experiences. For example, self-awareness may help us realize that we are anxious about an impending staff meeting. Self-empathy would then involve responding to that anxiety with kindness, perhaps by first acknowledging the difficulty of the situation and reminding ourselves that it is natural to be nervous.

Self-empathy does not necessarily follow from self-awareness; in fact, even the most self-aware people tend to respond to their feelings with judgment rather than caring. We must cultivate self-empathy through intentional practice and changes in our attitude toward ourselves.

In other words, self-awareness is the perception and recognition of ourselves, while self-empathy is the caring response to that perception. Both approaches work to improve mental and emotional well-being and personal growth, with self-awareness often being the forerunner of effective self-empathy. However, self-awareness does not make us self-empathetic; both traits must be developed to respond with kindness rather than harsh self-criticism.

Self-empathy involves noticing and acknowledging what is going on without buying into beliefs, assumptions, opinions, or judgments about our feelings. Using self-empathy may create space for empathizing with others and responding to ourselves with ethical responsibility and presence.

Self-empathy is an important and embodied competence in developing the capacity to experience empathy toward others. It may reduce projections and emotional contagion; hence, genuine empathy can exist and be helpful to others. At the same time, the development of self-empathy provides excellent grounds for emotional well-being, personal growth, and good relations with other people.

Caring involves noticing and being kind to ourselves by accepting experiences. Therefore, caring will present a supportive environment for learning without self-criticism and negativity amidst adversity, where there may be a prospect of failure. This may involve combining past and present experiences. In this way, we grow from these experiences without significant life changes. Again, the cultivation of self-empathy helps us understand others. It is a far more resilient approach to life.

Why is self-empathy necessary? Self-empathy gives another perspective to a world that is increasingly about success and productivity and less about mental and emotional well-being. Being fragile or vulnerable is not a weakness but one step toward healing and strength. This shift further helps to instill a strong foundation of positive self-regard and increases resiliency to face various life issues with patience and poise.

The road to self-empathy, simultaneously personal and social, should start with the realization that mistakes and setbacks are common experiences. This realization creates more considerate and supportive attitudes toward ourselves and others, improving our relationships and interactions with others. Accepting our failures allows us to extend such acceptance to others, creating a better, balanced, and harmonious organization.

Various studies have documented the powerful effect of self-empathy on mental health. One study involving over 3,000 participants discovered that self-empathy is associated with lower psychological distress, including worry, anxiety, and depression. It also encompasses life understanding and emotional well-being, thus indicating the power of self-empathy to create happiness and a high quality of life.

Some significant components of self-empathy include acknowledging and validating feelings during distress. For example, we could say, "It's all right to feel overwhelmed now. This is a difficult time, and it's all right to feel challenged." Self-empathy also means being gentle with ourselves when we have messed things up and recognizing needs that must be met. If we are experiencing self-doubt, choosing to practice self-forgiveness will release guilt or regret.

It's not about feeling superior. Instead, it's about understanding our thoughts and feelings neutrally and releasing ourselves from overwhelming self-criticism. Such understanding creates a positive spiral of empathy toward oneself and others, furthering better relationships and team dynamics.

It is essential that leaders develop self-empathy. This will boost self-awareness and resilience, contributing to authentic leadership. Leaders must understand and support their teams by adopting a gentle, nonjudgmental attitude toward self-thoughts, emotions, and experiences. This understanding empowers leaders on their professional journeys to create a collaborative and supportive environment, increasing morale and productivity.

Contrary to the myths perpetuated, self-empathy does not lower standards or breed sloth. According to science, self-empathy practitioners are much more self-aware, challenging, and genuine. They can understand others, creating a positive spiral of caring and hope. People with extensive self-criticism tend to be hostile, anxious, and depressed.

In other words, self-empathy is a potent means toward emotional balance, personal growth, and healthy interpersonal engagement. We can cultivate a spacious and receptive inner space by being present, integrating experiences with openness, and suspending judgment. We grow self-empathy to enrich our lives while making this world more empathetic and harmonious.

One of the most profound ways to navigate daily life is to manage tension and get things done. If we're attuned to what we bring into the situation, we can empathize with others. It's only when we go back within ourselves to our experience and acknowledge it that we can allow space for the experience and action of another.

Self-Compassion

Self-compassion means being kind, understanding, and caring toward ourselves — especially when we fail, we're hurting, or going through a difficult time. Why, so often, is a simple "yes" compared to gluttony or even cowardice rather than praised and trumpeted as one of our greatest tools to fortify our humanity and strength within the emotional world? Self-compassion is like a merger of the ancient practice of mindfulness and the vignette of psychology that we can use to chart a course through the hurdles of life with more ease and authenticity. Self-compassion is the only thing we know to turn to ourselves for a bit of encouragement — strength, balance, bonding. As Dr. Kristin Neff, an early pioneer in the study of self-compassion, put it: "Having compassion for yourself means that you honor and accept your humanness. No one is going to be on your side. You will not meet your standards; you will fail; you will mess up, hit your limits. It is the human condition, the universal reality of all of us."

It includes three interconnected components: self-kindness, common humanity, and mindfulness. It is that mixture of pampering we deserve the most after feeling hurt, much like one would do for the broom of their heart, the best kind of friend. Where cruel condemnation kicks in on error and misfortune, self-kindness creates caring and nuanced responses in supportive voices. Common humanity then follows, based on the realization that that actually is a human case. Every human has baggage, failures, shortcomings — every single one. Mindfulness asks us to do this with our feelings and experiences: be kind to them, not reactive, and not overwhelmed. Together, these three aspects form the basis of self-compassion, allowing people to make their way through life's highs and lows with greater clarity and ease.

The specific purpose of self-compassion might be to reduce self-criticism. We all have an interpreter — a voice focused on our faults, errors, and shortcomings. Even though self-criticism might seem to be something that motivates us to get the job done, it actually makes us more stressed, anxious, and depressed, according to studies. What we are in need of is self-compassion. When we engage in this act of compassion, we compel in ourselves an ecology of growth and learning rather than an ecology of shame and fear. We are not dismissing our flaws or living in some alternate universe in which we never have to answer for our actions, but instead acknowledging that we have these flaws and concluding that those flaws are the basis of our value. Putting our criticisms of self into being compassionate to self will make it more likely we will meet the challenges of this life with positivity and enjoyment.

Meanwhile, self-compassion will nurture emotional resilience, the resilience needed to face setbacks and adversity. At its extreme, life is really totally uncertain; everything changes in just a blink of an eye or a matter of a few seconds; no matter how well we plan our lives, it all can change because of a few life-changing events. From this standpoint, the practice of self-compassion, when we feel challenged, develops our interior resources to cope with life's fluctuations, highs, and lows. Research has shown that people with higher self-compassion have lower levels of anxiety and depression and higher levels of life satisfaction and emotional well-being. This is because self-compassion keeps us from the pitfalls of hardness and instead teaches us to feel our feelings without being definitively stuck there. It helps us to see barriers as challenges and chances to grow, as opposed to something impossible to overcome.

Another profoundly positive impact of self-compassion is that it appears to enhance motivation. Counterintuitive proof that self-compassion doesn't equal complacency — treating ourselves kindly actually incentivizes a growth mindset. If we create an environment in which we are free to fail and are not subject to harsh, uncaring self-criticism, we can more easily take risks and reach our goal(s). Self-compassion helps us gain insights from what went wrong rather than find ourselves frozen. One study published in the Journal of Personality and Social Psychology, for instance, found that, compared to those who employed self-critical strategies, self-compassionate people agreed more with the assertion that they were responsible for their mistakes and reported being more motivated to improve themselves. That in and of itself is a testament that self-compassion is not an excuse to let ourselves off the hook — it's an internal nurturing environment that actually enables evolution and growth.

It's also vital in developing far better personal relationships. How we treat ourselves is going to take care of a lot of the heavy lifting when it comes to treating others kindly. We do not make the mistake of kindness towards each other and get sour judgment for ourselves. That sort of imbalance breeds resentment, isolation, and burnout. When we work on self-compassion, we build an internal wealth that enriches our relationships. Further, self-compassion has been consistently found to be positively correlated with empathy, forgiveness, and emotional intelligence, which are essential for health and deepening relationships.

It's not always straightforward because many of us are used to self-criticism. However, this can be learned with practice. One highly effective tool is the "self-compassion break," created by Dr. Kristin Neff. In difficulty, take a breath and pay mindful attention to your pain. Tell yourself, "This is a moment of suffering." Then, call forth our common humanity and say, "Suffering is part of life." Then, incorporate words of kindness and support like, "May I be kind to myself in this moment" or "May I give myself the compassion I need." This will help us move from a judgment to a caring mindset, inner peace, and connection.

Journaling is another tool to promote self-compassion. Spend time examining what we experienced, and write to ourselves as we would to a best friend. What might we offer as advice to a close friend in the same situation? This practice may help us shift to a kinder mindset about ourselves. Mindfulness meditation and deep breathing can also help us stay with our feelings and not get swept away by them. We do not expect ourselves to be perfect, and we let our practice of self-compassion take root slowly.

Finally, self-compassion and compassion practices can change our relationship with ourselves and our world. Reorient towards kindness, common humanity, and mindfulness, and the ground is thus turned and cultivated for emotional resilience, personal growth, and interconnected relationships to act as a forest undergrowth in our lives. Thus, self-compassion in any way does not point out weakness; rather, it's a powerful resource for us to get all our strengths to confront difficult times joyfully. Many journeys end with a place; keeping its maintenance is a self-compassionate journey. This doesn't happen by magic or wishes; we can grow into a more compassionate relationship with ourselves, allowing forgiveness that improves our lives in ways we never imagined possible.

"Do you love me?" Alice asked.

"No, I don't love you," replied the White Rabbit.

Alice frowned and clasped her hands together,
as she did when she was hurt.

"See?" replied the White Rabbit.

"Now you will start asking yourself what makes you flawed and
what you did to make me not love you, not even a little bit.

You know, that's why I don't love you. You won't always be loved, Alice.

There will be times when other people are tired and bored
with life, when their heads are in the clouds, and they'll hurt
you. Because people are like that, they'll always hurt each
other's feelings in some way. Sometimes it's because of their
carelessness, sometimes it's because of their misunderstandings, and
sometimes it's because of their own conflicts with themselves.

If you don't love yourself a bit, if you don't armor yourself
with self-love and happiness, even the smallest irritations

that others inflict on you will be fatal and damaging.

When I first saw you, I made a deal with myself: 'I will refrain from

loving you until you love yourself."

~ Lewis Carrol,
"Alice in Wonderland"

Isn't Self-Loving Just Narcissism in Another Form?

Self-love and narcissism, at a glance, could seem to be one and the same, but when we dig into the roots, expressions, and rationale for their existence, they seem to be different animals altogether. Self-love in and of itself is a way of showing and feeling real, positive feelings for ourselves through self-respect, self-esteem, and the way we exist in a particular manner that recognizes our value. It's accepting our strengths and weaknesses, loving the things we don't love about ourselves, and being sweet to ourselves. It helps us flourish and return to our homeostatic state when we practice self-love. It teaches us to establish healthy boundaries, self-care, and keep our relationships with others safe. It is not self-indulgent; it allows space for empathy and rapport, and it gives rise to a stable sense of self-esteem that is independent of worthy validation from others.

In contrast, narcissism is characterized by the excessive desire to be treated as important, the need for admiration, and a lack of consideration and compassion for others. What might be concealed behind this facade of bravado is yet again something insecure and insignificant, thus needing to raise oneself by lowering others. Self-love, on the other hand, does not rely on attention from others, comparisons to others, or the need to belittle others to feel validated. Narcissists can hardly build intimate connections, giving their energy to creating the facade of idealism instead of bonds.

However, the most significant difference between these mindsets is the motivations behind them and their results. Self-love is inward-looking; it builds self-acceptance and ownership. This helps empower people to confront challenges with humility and grace, as when our self-worth is compartmentalized outside of achievement and applause, nothing can rattle us. Narcissism, by contrast, is outward-facing, requiring others to buttress a grandiose self-image. It breeds defensiveness, entitlement, and insensitivity to the feelings or needs of others. Self-love balances relationships and promotes harmony, whereas narcissism causes discord, manipulation, and unequal respect.

A second significant difference lies in the relationship of these concepts to vulnerability. Self-love accepts vulnerability as part of humanity. It allows one to recognize errors, seek assistance, and grow and learn from experiences. Narcissism, in contrast, denies vulnerability, sometimes substituting arrogance or defensiveness. However, any acceptance of their flaws or response to constructive criticism threatens the fragile self-image that narcissists maintain through an arsenal of covering behaviors, and this leads to a failure to form a new or updated solution. The inability to process vulnerability can limit personal development and ruin relationships.

This self-care may parallel narcissism on the outside by centering around the self, but where true self-love comes from a person's inner foundations of honesty and authenticity, narcissism lies in the ego. Self-love is a healthy, loving view of oneself that nurtures well-being and relationships. Narcissism, on the other hand, is born out of insecurity, with excessive emphasis on getting external validation and being better than others, usually at their expense. Self-love comes from humility, empathy, and self-awareness; narcissism relies on denial, entitlement, and superficiality. This distinction is key for developing true self-worth and real relationships with others.

Self-Loving

Saying "loving" rather than "love" makes the concept an active project rather than just a feeling or mode of being; loving suggests intention and practice. When we describe a person as loving, the word attests to their active decisions: to care for, show kindness, express fondness, and love in motion. It transforms love from an abstraction into a living, dynamic force that needs attention and effort. As Erich Fromm contended in The Art of Loving, love is not a random feeling that befalls us but a deliberate act — an art that requires effort and intention. "Loving" embraces this continuous action, reminding us that relationships are not just there but deepened, and their roots are nourished through active and deliberate acts of love. It reimagines love as active and participatory, a choice in every moment that nourishes our connections and deepens our shared humanity. It's a reminder that love is not just a feeling but an act of doing; therefore, "loving" is one very important and life-changing ritual in our day-to-day lives.

Self-loving is the conscious act of appreciation and cherishing ourselves, recognizing our uniqueness and value. It is more than pampering ourselves and buying new clothes for ourselves. While treating ourselves may be a part of self-love, it's way more significant than that. It's a daily, committed practice to treat yourself as someone who is worthy of love, respect, and kindness.

This might feel strange or even selfish, perhaps in a world where a person's value is usually marked by productivity, external achievement, or the measure against another. But the truth is self-loving is not self-centered and is not self-important; it is preparation for personal health, emotional endurance, and genuine engagement with others. Psychologist Deborah Khoshaba states that self-love is the state of gratefulness for oneself that grows from actions that support our physical, psychological, and spiritual growth. It is a practice that allows us to live more authentically.

At its core, self-loving begins with self-acceptance. It means embracing our strengths, our weaknesses, our edges — the things about ourselves that we feel are more vulnerable or less than perfect. That does not mean coasting or pretending we do not have work to do — gaps in our goals; it means realizing we are not terrible and should not be "perfect" and hit our milestones to be worthy. Acceptance of ourselves provides a basis of belonging and inner security. As a result, this inner stability will push us to be bolder in life's troubles! Studies indicate those who score high in self-acceptance have higher levels of happiness and emotional stability and less labeling of anxiety and/or depression than other individuals.

Requiring love also means creating limits and placing needs first. Most people find it hard to say "no" as they fear others might feel disappointed or that relationships might suffer. But not doing so creates resentment, burnout, and low self-worth. Self-loving means knowing your time, energy, and peace of mind are valuable and worth defending. This means maybe saying no to a commitment when it is too much to bear, discussing your needs when they are not being met, and/or making room for rest and self-care in everyday life. Setting boundaries is not a selfish venture. It is an undertaking of respect to our being. As Brené Brown presents, "Daring to set boundaries is about having the courage to love ourselves even when we risk disappointing and upsetting other people."

The second key is to build a positive inner dialogue, a kind one. The way we talk to ourselves affects mental and emotional well-being. However, for many, developing an inner critic acts to exaggerate their flaws and downplay their achievements. This kind of self-talk can erode self-esteem and instill inadequate feelings. In self-loving, we dislodge the inner critic and bottle-feed the inner ally: a soothing, supportive, and sympathetic inner voice. Instead of focusing on what is missing, self-loving encourages us to celebrate our strengths and to appreciate our growth, however small. Studies show that repeating positives can help improve self-esteem, reduce tension, and improve overall well-being.

As such, self-loving also implies awareness and celebration of our self-worth, which does not rely upon external things. In our modern world, separating self-worth from accomplishments, looks, or how others perceive us is tricky. However, true self-loving is not reliant upon the outside; it is internal. This worthiness is the same as our intrinsic aliveness, which belongs in a vacuum that no one else can fulfill. That freedom can be hugely liberating: it can lift constant needs to prove ourselves to ourselves and others. As Louise Hay said, "You've been criticizing yourself for years, and it hasn't worked. Give yourself approval and see what happens.

Self-loving is a personal experience that impacts our interactions with other beings. If we let others know how we want to be treated, we can replace any negative beliefs about ourselves, which will set the standard for others on how to treat us. We will be more apt to attract people who will relate to us in a respectful, mindful, and values-based way and maintain relationships with them. Plus, it increases our ability to love other people. However, when our own vessel is brimming, we can give the best part of ourselves — the most generous offerings of our energy and heart, without fear of running dry. Alternatively, lacking self-loving often results in codependence, people-pleasing, or seeking outside validation. When we practice self-loving, we forge the strongest version of ourselves, with which we can engage in relationships from a place of authenticity and mutual respect.

Self-care habits are deliberate and will require practice, particularly if we've been hard on ourselves and/or neglected our needs in the past. One of the most valuable ways to practice self-love is daily affirmations. Try starting with the following daily affirmations: "I deserve loving and respect" or "I am whole just as I am." Repeating those positive affirmations helps us gradually eliminate the negative mental process and build confidence. Self-compassion meditations, where you send love and kindness to ourselves — especially during challenging times — are a very powerful practice. Another equally powerful exercise can be imagining ourselves as our younger self and then giving that younger version of ourselves unconditional loving.

Another effective tool for self-loving is journaling. Spend some time noticing the things we like about ourselves, what we have achieved, and what makes us special. Writing Letters to Myself: A Journey of Struggles, Resilience ties us more into our innards and is also a written document of self-loving we can look back on when life gets hard. Read uplifting books, only talk to supportive friends, and follow the role models that will constantly lead us to self-loving.

There is no destination in being more self-loving; it's a continuous process of honoring and caring for ourselves. It is a commitment to loving, being kind, and respecting ourselves. We build a life that is in harmony with who we are through self-acceptance, healthy boundaries, positive self-talk, and valuing ourselves. Self-loving will change our lives, relationships, and how we show ourselves to the world. On our way to self-loving perfection has nothing to do with authenticity — it has everything to do with our progress, patience, and courage to take ourselves fully. In time and with intention, self-loving can be the base upon which a rich, fulfilling life, ours alone, will stand.

CHAPTER 8

Wisdom and Purpose

Simply put, our heart's wisdom is necessarily knitted into our purposes. It is that still, quiet voice inside that urges us to authenticity, fullness, and connection. Our heart does not measure life by awards or even achievements — but it does request meaning, joy, and alignment to what feels true. In a world that so frequently defines success in terms of external markers — titles, wealth, productivity — it is easy to forget to listen to that inner wisdom. We may pursue aims that leave us hollow inside, detached from the deeper truths our souls would have us live by.

Our purpose is not something society tells us or forces us to do; it is a very personal thing and something that is already inside us. It is not often high-minded or itself furled around a single ambition. Instead, it is embroidered in the small, quiet moments that bring us to life — a conversation that sustains us, a chore that energizes us, and an unobtrusive sense of satisfaction after alleviating the plight of someone in need. Our heart's wisdom doesn't require our purpose to be grand; only our purpose should be real. It asks us to listen, to pay attention, to believe what seems precious, even if it falls outside the world's sense of its value.

Now is the time to step back into our hearts' deeper desires — the ones that might have been lost amidst decades of achieving and serving others or moving toward journeys that did not resonate with our essence. What gives pleasure? What brings life and activates passion? When are we most alive? These are our heart's clues to an aligned and on-target life.

Joy is among the clearest signals from our heart. Not the ecstatic joy of outward reward, but deep, vibrant joy, a satisfaction born not from some resultant engagement but from a deeper engagement in something that's just right. It could be creative engagement, engagement in the context of an intimate relationship, or serving other people in a way that's aligned with our values. Joy says, "This is it; this is where we need to be." It brings us closer to our purpose whenever we act in its direction. Seeking joy is not selfish — our compass guides us to live the life meant for us.

Passion, too, is a guide. Passion is the essence of our soul ignited when we discover what gets us fired up. Passions don't always arrive as this big-blaring, single-fit-all driving force; they can show up in the quieter, more profound things we care about, the problems we need to address, etc. What is important, where are we willing to spend our time and energy, is often our passion. As such, by pursuing these things that ignite passion within us, our decisions align with the principles and values most deeply embedded within our hearts.

But purpose isn't only about following joy and passion — it's also about service. The wisdom of our hearts often beckons us out of ourselves to question how we can put something back of value into the world and make a difference in the lives of others. That does not mean sacrificing our needs or ignoring our dreams; instead, it means understanding that the most rewarding causes we can have in our lives are related to something larger than ourselves. With a heart as home, it would say it this way: our relationships, creation, lanes of teaching and learning, looking after someone that we care about, and social movements that we think all give way to connecting to the people around us. Our purpose of connecting becomes a wholesomeness of serving others better for the greater good.

Of course, it isn't easy to trust our heart's guidance. Its arc is rarely linear or predictable; it may invite us to take risks, release old beliefs or expectations, and walk into the unknown. It might call on us to confront our fears, trust in ourselves, and go in a direction that others can't quite get. But our heart's values don't care what anyone else thinks; it's about what is true for us. By living our values and trusting the unfolding path, we start to create a life full of meaning and one that is incredibly genuine to who we are.

Identify the barriers that separate us from experiencing meaning in our lives and how to transcend them. The fear, self-doubt, and pressure to conform suffocate our heart's voice. However, by fostering self-empathy, self-compassion, and self-loving practices, we can start to quiet the noise and listen to our inner direction more clearly. Purpose is not a destination — it is a practice, a state of being. It is something we find and will find repeatedly as we grow and continue to grow.

Ultimately, this is not about perfection or being done but about building a life that feels congruent with who we are inside. It's about being intentional, ensuring we are doing what's important to us, and trusting that it will take us there little by little. Guidance from the wisdom of our hearts is always available — we only need to listen.

Take a moment to consider what matters. Allow dreams and imagination to see without any type of judgment or limitation. Since purpose can't be forced or faked, it already exists, just waiting to be found. The more we practice leading with our hearts, the more our lives will feel charged, meaningful, and joy-filled. It's a gift of dwelling in the frequency that aligns with our purpose: a life that feels not only full but verifiable ours.

This is very personal and transformative work. As alignment with our heart's purpose arises, it demands self-awareness and, when done well, a willingness to risk vulnerability that comes with growth. Searching and living a heart purpose has reflective, connecting, and active elements. Guidance from thought leaders and researchers tells us these are key steps we can take along our journey toward fulfillment with what lies in our heart as our purpose.

Discovering our heart's purpose — commonly known as discovering our "true calling" or "soul's purpose" — will require questions, reflections, deliberation, and alignment with our values. That journey often starts with self-inquiry. Questions to ask ourselves: What makes me happy? What feels meaningful to me? What activities do I lose track of time doing? The specific questions will turn up intrinsic motivations and passions, which are just so connected to the purpose of our hearts.

According to psychiatrist and Holocaust survivor Viktor Frankl, meaning comes from pursuing goals beyond ourselves. In his seminal book *Man's Search for Meaning*, Frankl argued that purpose typically arises when we do meaningful work, develop deep connections with people, and confront the difficulties of life with brave hearts and a willful spirit. Looking back on our experiences and figuring out when we have been most fulfilled might provide valuable hints.

Another way is to listen to the needs of the world around us. Spiritual teacher Parker Palmer puts it this way: In his book *Let Your Life Speak*, he suggests purpose lies at the crossroads of what brings us joy and what the world needs. This means hearing that inner voice while listening to the world outside. Practices such as mindfulness, journaling, and meditation can quiet distractions and give way to authentic desires. It also enables us to see the work we accomplish and shows us where our unique qualities create change so that we can find our purpose in serving others.

Additional Approaches

Practical Implementation:

Bill Burnett and Dave Evans, in "Designing Your Life," recommend:
- Creating mind maps of possible paths
- Conducting "life design interviews" with people in fields that interest you
- Prototyping different experiences through volunteering or job shadowing
- Tracking your energy levels during different activities
- Testing assumptions through small experiments

Purpose Verification Framework:

According to Richard Leider's research:
- Gifts: Identify your inherent talents and acquired skills
- Passions: What moves you emotionally and intellectually
- Values: Your core beliefs and non-negotiables

- Place: Environments where you thrive
- Impact: The change you want to create

Obstacles and Challenges:

Common barriers identified by psychologist Robert Biswas-Diener include:

- Perfectionism and fear of choosing wrong
- External pressures and expectations
- Financial constraints
- Limited exposure to possibilities
- Fear of failure or judgment

Integration Strategies:

- Create a personal mission statement
- Develop a five-year vision with flexible markers
- Establish quarterly reviews of direction and progress
- Build a support network of mentors and accountability partners
- Practice regular reflection and adjustment

Psychological Perspectives:

Carl Jung's concept of individuation suggests purpose often emerges through:

- Shadow work (examining rejected aspects of self)
- Archetype exploration (understanding recurring patterns)
- Active imagination exercises
- Dream journaling and analysis

Wisdom Traditions:

Various spiritual and philosophical traditions offer complementary insights:

- Buddhist mindfulness practices for clarity
- Stoic exercises in perspective-taking
- Indigenous wisdom about connection to community and nature
- Contemporary contemplative practices

Modern Research Applications:

Recent studies in positive psychology suggest purpose development is enhanced by:

- Identifying and using signature strengths daily
- Building positive relationships
- Engaging in meaningful activities
- Pursuing achievable goals
- Finding ways to serve others

Listen to Your Inner Voice

Teaching purpose often comes through intuition and inner knowing. When we learn to listen to our inner voice, we are silencing what we have heard from outside sources and the society we live in that may have led us astray from what is our truth. Practices like mindfulness or meditation help us tune into this inner guidance. Brené Brown describes this as "wholehearted living," where we have the courage to let go of what will make others proud of us and instead seek only what feels true and valuable. The way to align with our true calling is to trust our intuition.

Peaceful time spent being with ourselves can help us recognize our truest desires. What is our intuition telling us? We could try a mindfulness practice in which we visualize our ideal life or ask ourselves how our hearts would feel when demands from others were removed.

Cultivate Gratitude and Presence

Ultimately, connecting with our heart's purpose means being present and enjoying life's journey. Gratitude keeps us steady and connected to what is essential. By celebrating the small wins on the way, we affirm to ourselves, time and again, that we live a life true to ourselves. According to the positive psychology developed by Robert Emmons, gratitude has effects that build emotional well-being and connect a person deeper with purpose.

Aligning with our heart's purpose is a holistic journey that mixes self-reflection, emotional courage, and meaningful action. We identify our values, listen to our intuition, and embrace vulnerability, and we create a life that aligns deeply with our authentic selves. This journey is not about doing things perfectly, but it is about doing things progressively — continuing to expand on your unique contribution to the world.

CHAPTER 9

Safe Leadership Boundaries

The Power of Safe Leadership Boundaries

Leadership boundaries are not walls; they are pathways. They iconically balance professionalism and humanity, authority, and accessibility. When properly defined and consistently implemented, these boundaries create trust, clarity, and respect for each other within a team organization. They keep the relationships strong, the expectations clear, and the integrity intact. Leaders appreciate how boundaries are not there to stifle possibility but to provide a safe context for people to be their best selves. Action without boundaries often becomes a reaction instead of an intention. Even in the best of situations, members of teams tend to have overlapping roles, expectations that are difficult to outline, and goals that are misaligned. Team members might feel unsupported or undervalued, and the leaders themselves might burn out trying to swim through the chaos. In contrast, safe leadership boundaries lead to clarity and confidence. They establish a structure whereby all parties know their purpose and responsibilities, which leads to more seamless interaction, better collaboration, and improved productivity.

Finding the Balance Between Connection and Professionalism

A major challenge of leadership is balancing connection with professionalism. One key responsibility of leaders is to build solid relationships with their followers — listening to their worries, addressing their needs, and offering assistance. However, personal and professional relationships need to be progressed with caution. Leaders who cross that line into their employees' personal lives can risk their authority and muddy the waters of their role.

To provide an example, a leader who shares a lot of personal experience with their teams might unknowingly reverse the roles, making it hard for team members to see them as a strong guiding force. Conversely, a leader who is too in touch with all an employee's personal struggles may lack the perspective to make sound decisions or give objective feedback. Safe boundaries allow leaders to remain empathetic and supportive without venturing into territory that might compromise their professional stature or the team's togetherness. This balance applies to how leaders conduct team-building or informal get-togethers with employees. Building camaraderie and a sense of belonging is essential, but leaders need to be cautious of what kinds of events are in the social or informal setting. In doing so, they show respect for their position and the business aspect of the relationships among the team.

The Ripple Effect of Clear Expectations

Clear expectations create the foundation of safe leadership bounds. When leaders spell out what they expect regarding behavior, performance, and communication, they set a foundation for accountability and respect. The expectations give guidelines the team members will use to work with each other while ensuring transparency and fostering trust among team members.

For example, a leader who preaches work-life balance but sets no boundaries around emails and after-hours communication doesn't just undermine their message; they demonstrate what the organization truly values. Likewise, a leader who sets specific boundaries for constructive critique fosters an environment in which team members feel comfortable sharing ideas or reservations because those people feel secure in doing so without fear of being judged or punished. While these boundaries help mitigate disequilibrium, they also enable people to take ownership of their work and their contribution to the success of the team itself.

Additionally, clear expectations provide a framework for overcoming struggles or disputes. Since everyone has clear expectations, it encourages problem-solving and resolution. With this clarity, team members can focus on their goals and responsibilities, confident they are supported by a leader committed to fairness and consistency.

Emotional Boundaries: Strong and Calm Always

Emotional boundaries are a key but often ignored leadership tool. Leaders often face emotionally charged situations, whether to work through interpersonal disagreements, team challenges, or even their own stress. Without healthy emotional boundaries, leaders can either react to their team's emotions or hold them inside, neither of which will help them be effective — or even get out of bed at the beginning of the day. Safe emotional boundaries allow leaders to act mindfully and not just react reflexively. For instance, a leader who stays calm in a team conflict sets a tone for a respectful and solution-oriented dialogue. Modeling emotional regulation also establishes stability and trust, with team members reassured that issues can be resolved in a constructive way.

Simultaneously, emotional boundaries shield leaders from being overwhelmed by the stress or emotions of others. This does not prevent leaders from being detached or unfeeling; it just means they need to balance empathy and self-preservation. Leaders who internalize their team's stress as their own will eventually experience burnout, rendering them unable to offer the support and guidance their team so desperately needs. Emotional boundaries enable leaders to be empathetic and engaged without sacrificing their own mental health.

Ethical Leadership: A Fundamental Boundary

To lead either safely or effectively, ethical limits are absolute. They function as a compass, helping leaders to plot a course that is equitable, transparent, and resonates with the organization's principles. They safeguard against favoritism, conflict of interest, and breaches of confidentiality, so trust is not put at risk. Ethical leaders are honest; honesty creates trust — a crucial component when fostering credibility and respect in the workplace. A leader who is prudent and sensitive to information develops and cultivates trust in their leadership in their team. In the same vein, when leaders set expectations of accountability for themselves and their teams when it comes to ethical practices, they create a culture of fairness.

Decision-making is also about ethical lines. This is a type of power dynamic where leaders must often make tough decisions by balancing competing priorities. The function of leaders is to make these impactful choices while demonstrating moral fulfillment and respect for their responsibilities. This integrity builds the leader's credibility and serves as a strong example for the team.

Time Boundaries: A Culture of Respect and Balance

Setting times is another core aspect of safe leadership. In a time when technology erases boundaries between life and work, leaders need to be intentional about honoring their team's time. This involves setting realistic expectations around working hours, promoting breaks, and respecting personal time. Since time can't be bought back, a leader who decides to refrain from sending out late-night emails or scheduling meetings during lunch breaks gives their group a heads-up that they value their time. Such a culture of sustainability is built on such respect for boundaries — a sense of clear boundaries that allows employees to prioritize their well-being without feeling judged.

Time boundaries should also be set for the leader's own calendar. Overextending themselves risks burnout and hampers their ability to lead effectively. When leaders set limits on their availability, they not only model healthy behavior but also show others what balance looks like. This not only helps the leader but also strengthens the organization's focus on employee well-being.

Basics of Empowered Leadership

Safe leadership boundaries do not limit; they free. They develop a culture where people can give their best, confident in the knowledge that they are enabled within a framework of trust, mutual respect, and accountability. Leaders maintain psychological safety by not taking things personally, clearly explaining their intentions, controlling emotions, being ethical, and respecting time.

These boundaries enable leaders to engage with their integrity and purpose and create a culture where people feel valued and capable of thriving. These are the cornerstones of empathetic, ethical, and effective leadership; make no mistake; these are not mere guides. Formidable leaders who embrace these boundaries will catapult innovation, collaboration, and growth seamlessly within their teams and organizations. After all, safe leadership isn't about the actions of the leaders themselves; it's about how they set the stage for health and flourishing in the people around them.

CHAPTER 10

Leading from Our Heart

Reawakening to heart truth is not a destination but the journey of a lifetime. And just like anything else, it's a practice that happens moment to moment, choice to choice, as we navigate the ebb and flow of life. While the linear paths we are encouraged to take lead to a linear destination, living from our heart is a spiral process that continues to evolve. Of course, there will be times when we experience such clear and profound awareness that we feel our heart speak within us, while at other times, self-doubt, fear, and/or pain will blur our intuition. That, again, would be natural: a journey of our heart is never a journey of perfection; instead, it's one of persistence — a willingness to go in now and then, despite it all, continue.

If we lead from that space within our heart, we embrace all that life presents: the beauty and the ugliness, the good and the bad. That means being authentically present, even when that is difficult. That means being with intense feelings, at times painfully challenging ones. That means trusting the wisdom we carry in a more profound place can support whatever comes up for us in our hearts. Wisdom of our heart isn't automatic; it is the consequence of devotion to self-compassion and the deliberate will to listen to that internal whispering voice of our heart amid all the cacophony around the world. It evolves at a pace with which living develops into an accustomed, steadying compass that settles us with our own self-evident truth.

Of all the heart-opening practices we will ever do, one of the most powerful involves gratitude. Gratitude is a perspective rather than just an emotion. It's a style or way of looking out through a pair of lenses on abundance versus scarcity. We start to see what we are thankful for instead of what we don't have; thus, we can open up our hearts and let life's abundant richness come in. Gratitude does not ask us to bypass pain or declare the world perfect; it simply reminds us of the beauty of simple moments we may have taken for granted and provides an invitation to hold both the tragic and the ecstatic. We can start a simple gratitude practice by reviewing our day and writing down three things for which we are grateful. With time, this practice shifts our attention so that we may plunge more profoundly into the present moment and the wisdom of our hearts.

Leading with gratitude refers to recognizing and valuing the effort, contribution, and presence of others in the organization, team, or community. It is not just an act; it is a practice or mindset that promotes connection, trust, and inspiration. For example, scientific studies in positive psychology conducted by Robert Emmons have shown that gratitude improves emotional health, strengthens relationships and sensitivity, and increases resilience. Leaders who practice gratitude as part of their leadership style build a culture of appreciation, which catalyzes personal and organizational development.

One of the most significant advantages of leading with gratitude is that it helps build relationships and instills trust. When a leader lets employees know they are valued as individuals, it portrays appreciation. Recognized employees are more engaged and invested in their work. A Gallup study has shown that employees who feel valued by their leaders are less likely to leave the organization by 56% and are more productive and satisfied than others. Expressing gratitude builds a bond, laying a foundation of trust that encourages collaboration and engagement.

Grateful leaders don't just focus on the things that are wrong or could be better — they shine a light on the good things and successes of their team members. Instead of using criticism, we can use positive reinforcement. This strengths-based, leader-centric perspective aligns with the work of Donald Clifton and Marcus Buckingham, who advocated for focusing on individuals and their talents that can contribute to more significant efforts. Recognizing the distinctive strengths of individual talents instills confidence in leaders and cultivates a sense of ownership and pride among team members for their work.

Being thankful and leading with gratitude guides us to resilience during difficult times. While gratitude does not eliminate challenges, it offers a spirit that allows leaders and groups to work through hardship with hope and resolve. Gratitude for forward movement, no matter how measly, is part of a Growth Mindset, as noted by Carol Dweck. With this mentality, we develop persistence and flexibility as we help teams learn from failure and stay focused on outcomes. Modeling gratitude in challenging times, leaders signal the value in finding lessons and opportunities in every experience, encouraging our teams to follow suit.

So, one big theme of gratitude in leadership is cultivating an appreciative culture. When leaders model expressing appreciation, a tone is established for how team members treat one another. The upward flow of gratitude runs through the organization and operating bodies, helping to foster the learning, cooperation, kindness, respect, and support that are the key ingredients in a learning environment. Adam Grant, an organizational psychologist, has found that gratitude increases prosocial behavior: helping, mentoring, and volunteering. When leaders weave gratitude into the workplace threads, a culture is created that inspires people to show up as their best selves, knowing they are seen, valued, and encouraged to give their utmost.

Yes, to lead with gratitude, leaders need to live it authentically and consistently. Authenticity is critical, however, because empty and hollow expressions of gratitude will erode trust rather than build it. Take the time to recognize each team member for unique contributions and personal efforts. Instead of general praise, for example, a leader can say, "I really appreciate how you stayed late last week to finalize the project. Your commitment made a tremendous impact." Specific and meaningful acknowledgments will show that gratitude is genuine and thoughtful.

Consistency is just as important. Gratitude is not an interval between breaks; it is cultivated in between the breaks we take. For example, leaders can build gratitude into their routines by promoting meetings focused on acknowledgments, sending thank-you notes, or taking a moment each day to consider what individuals on their team contribute. Such small but regular gestures cultivate a culture of gratitude with long-lasting positive impacts. According to Brené Brown, gratitude is not to be practiced in big moments but to become aware of what we appreciate, and mentioning it is daily practice.

Leading with gratitude is a practice that changes our conversations, improves our relationships, builds our psyche, and increases our mood. It brings leadership away from a transactional style toward one based on connection, recognition, and appreciation. Grateful leadership empowers others and cultivates an environment of trust, collaboration, and shared purpose. As Robert Emmons has pointed out, gratitude isn't just an emotion but a style of perception and interaction in the world — one that, in leadership, is an extraordinary catalyst for positive change.

Another leadership practice involved in leading from the heart is mindfulness — the art of being present. In our distraction-heavy world, losing contact with ourselves, getting caught up in the day's tasks, and forgetting to pause is so easy. Mindfulness is one way to encourage us to slow down, check in, and see what is happening with our thoughts, feelings, and sensations without judgment. It does so by allowing room for the wisdom of our heart to rise — something that can respond to life rather than react to it. We don't have to meditate for hours and hours; it's the little things, the simple things, breathing a couple of deep breaths before the beginning of the day, the warmth of the cup in our hands when we drink our coffee, even really listening to someone when they speak. These little seconds of presence remind us to return to our hearts and know what is essential and what we want.

Of course, heart-centered leading does not mean bypassing tests or feeling denial. As a truism, our heart often grows through challenges. When we encounter setbacks, instead of stuffing our feelings or willing our way through them, we can instead avail ourselves of self-compassion. Practicing self-compassion is treating ourselves with the same kindness and understanding we would give a dear friend.

That is, being okay with our pain, not self-judging, reminding us that it's OK to struggle, and giving grace to our hearts as life goes up and down. When we approach ourselves with self-compassion, we create a safe space to process our feelings, learn from our failures, and progress boldly and courageously.

Another path to leadership wisdom is a life of intentional living: making choices and taking action in alignment with what matters as much as possible. To do this, we are compelled to answer for ourselves:

- What does matter most to me?
- Who do I want to be as a leader?
- What are some ways that I can incorporate more of my values into my daily routine?

Intentional living allows us to return to leading with our hearts in a way that feels right and brings fulfillment to our lives. We can do this by setting boundaries for our capacity, committing time to a passion project, or just being better humans to those with whom we work.

The wisdom of our heart encourages us to connect, not to stay locked in, but to enter into that space of community and compassion. To begin, we must honestly assess for ourselves:

- How do I show up in my relationships?
- How do I show up broadly in the world?
- Do I spend time in and on relationships that uplift and inspire?
- Do I spend time with people who see and celebrate my authentic self?
- Do I see and celebrate others' authentic selves?
- When I hit challenges, do I ask my community for help or support?

To lead with heart is not to bear the weight of the world on our shoulders; it is to realize the power of human connection and interdependence.

Finally, we must allow ourselves to believe in the cyclical nature of this process. At times, it feels like we are one with our hearts, that all is flowing like water. At other times, we might feel lost and disconnected. Both are parts of the process. And, in those times when we are struggling, we need to go back to the practices that ground us: gratitude, mindfulness, self-compassion, and purpose-driven leading. We can trust that the wisdom of our hearts is still inside us, even if muted. The more we focus on this connection, the stronger and stronger we will be and the better aligned we will become.

Leading from our hearts is not about perfectionism or having all the answers. It's the daily grind of simply showing up with courage, honesty, and a willingness to listen. It means trusting that the knowledge our hearts hold is so vast that we cannot be misled down a path we cannot yet see. It emphasizes placing the quest — the unifying of the head and heart — not at its conclusion but in the journey itself: the messy, beautiful, and imperfect process of leading in which the wisdom of our hearts truly comes alive.

As we continue the wisdom of our heart's journeys, it is imperative that we continue to carry these practices. We let go of the need to make it all fit or be sensible and trust that we will find the way. In leading from our hearts, we create authentic lives and encourage others to do the same. Honor the wisdom of our heart, which becomes an ever-more-abundant gift. Live fully, love lots, and lead from within: this is where our greatest potential lies.

CHAPTER 11

The Role of Vulnerability in Leadership

In leading, vulnerability might just be that which most greatly revolutionizes how we connect, inspire, and lead our teams. It is also something almost indefinably brave for some, in some of those situations, to go through. There is one problem: it too often gets lumped in with the fragile and weak because it means merely the willingness to be vulnerable to be fully present, unfiltered, and without any barriers in a manner that allows connection. The vulnerable leader shows up as human and shows he or she is no better than being in a struggle, uncertainty, and imperfection. As such, it inspires the members of his team to connect to their authenticity and interact with work and their colleagues deeply in an authentic way. "Vulnerability is not about winning or losing; it's having the courage to show up and be seen when you have no control over the outcome." Dr. Brené Brown. Great leaders practice highly effective leading: they lead, they are vulnerable — a model, an amount that calls courage to bring the whole self into work — a breeding culture for trust, innovation, and resiliency.

The single most important upside to vulnerability in leadership, in my view, is trust. No team or organization will ever be successful without authenticity. When leaders are vulnerable, they rhyme their teams and inform them that they are not hiding behind some veneer of perfection or invincibility but allow themselves to be seen as if they truly are flawed, learning, and trying. For instance, a leader who admits to a mistake or confesses uncertainty in a difficult situation sends a powerful message to the team that honesty is more important than pretending to be in control. This kind of transparency earns trust because it shows the leader values integrity over ego. According to Kouzes and Posner, such traits are not perceived as frailties but have come to be accepted as hallmarks of leadership, for which leaders who "show their weaknesses" stand out as more forthright, reachable, and accessible, thus making much stronger bonds that attach leaders and their teams together. Trust, in turn, helps smoothen the operations of the team, improve communication flow, and help people view challenges with greater confidence.

Equally valuable for establishing psychological safety within the team is the condition of vulnerability. According to Amy Edmondson, psychological safety describes "a shared belief that it is safe to take risks and be direct (even with the possibility of rejection or penalty)." Leaders who claim their own vulnerabilities — whether by acknowledging they have no clue how to solve a problem, by revealing their own struggles, or by asking for help — encourage team members to do the same and provide the psychological safety to keep this dialogue open. Openness flattens hierarchies and crowdsources assistance, permission, and access so that employees may speak up, try new thinking, and learn from the failures accompanying experimentation without the fear of ridicule. For instance, a leader who is vulnerable to explain how they overcame a previous failure is normalizing not only failure but also, at the same time, inspiring their team to see mistakes as growth opportunities rather than career-ending moves. It's a springboard for creativity, innovation, and constant improvement.

The second dimension of vulnerability in leadership is in its ability to create emotional connection. It means that by being transparent with their teams, leaders are not just the people leading them to do strategic efforts but real, feeling individuals who know their efforts are worth caring for. For example, acknowledging the emotional toll of a challenging project or showing appreciation for their team's effort is one way a leader can recognize that team members are people, not just employees. The emotional bonding by organizations strengthens their loyalty and morale, making team members feel valued and understood. However, as far as leaders are concerned, they should be tactful in revealing personal struggles or feelings. Vulnerability in leadership is not about oversharing or burdening your team with your emotional well-being; it's about showing up to be human in a manner that inspires connection and builds trust. As Brown points out, vulnerability involves "engaging in meaningful connection" — it's not about losing sight of professional boundaries.

When leaders are vulnerable, they also are humble, which is a key part of effective leadership. Leader humility has oftentimes involved the realization and acceptance that no one has all the answers and that leadership is a continual process of learning and development for everyone. Vulnerable leaders are never afraid to say they are wrong, ask for feedback from their team members, and ask for help when needed. This humility not only enhances the leader's credibility but inspires team members to pitch in, take initiative, and own their functions.

In their work on feedback, Sheila Heen and Douglas Stone emphasize this idea further. They point out that when leaders are open to constructive criticism, they create a culture of respect and mutual trust where employees feel valued and heard. In this case, vulnerability isn't weakness; it's strength — the strength to choose learning and collaboration over ego. Besides, vulnerability creates team resilience during times of uncertainty or crisis.

Leaders can build solidarity and a sense of purpose within their teams through acknowledgments of their teams' challenges, besides sharing their own feelings and concerns. For instance, during the COVID-19 pandemic, many of the leaders who leaned into vulnerability manifested their humanness with the difficulties they had to be away from work by showing connectedness with the problems faced by their employees and supporting them wherever they could. This built team cohesion and confirmed that leadership is about helping others excel, not just about delivering a result. In this sense, vulnerability becomes an instrument of connection between leaders and their teams, and it is a tool for resilience when things get tough.

Vulnerability creates connection, builds trust, and drives inclusion in leadership. By being transparent about their limitations or challenges, leaders can level the playing field in their teams, tearing down hierarchical barriers and ensuring every voice is heard. This is particularly important within diverse teams since background, experience, or perspective differences might inadvertently create power imbalances. Vulnerable leaders also show that leading does not mean knowing everything but making room for collaboration and co-decision-making.

Catalyst reported that being a vulnerable leader in facilitating belonging and inclusion is what characterizes top leaders in team performance and innovation. Most importantly, vulnerability in leadership is a great way to activate authenticity and courage at the team level. When leaders show up as their authentic selves — unafraid to share their weaknesses, doubts, or feelings — they grant their team members permission to share the same. Such an approach fosters a culture of authenticity when people are comfortable voicing ideas, taking risks, and having their whole selves present at work. Vulnerable leaders give others courage by showing what leading with integrity and heart looks like. These leaders remind us that outstanding leadership is not about being invulnerable but being brave enough to be authentic in ways that scare us and may hurt or be risky.

Let me put it all together: vulnerability is the foundation of good leadership. Therein lies the power of vulnerability: in showing that, as leaders, we are but human, we are courageous, humble, and empathetic, thus creating an environment where psychological safety, innovation, and collaboration can thrive. Leaders learn that vulnerability involves reaching out to every human being in the team in a way that engages the effort of mutual loyalty, resilience, and collective purpose. As research increasingly points to the power of vulnerability in leadership, the evidence is clear: it's not those who lead from invulnerability that are most effective; it's those who lead from within themselves.

Coming Home to Ourselves

In the wisdom of our hearts, we do not find this wisdom outside of ourselves or in anything beyond ourselves. It is not to be discovered like a secret or place to arrive at. It is already here, in us, waiting for us to stop, quiet the noise, and listen. It doesn't require us to make grand displays of feeling or all the right moves in the proper order. Our heart knows what it knows and speaks the truth gently and steadily in its revolution. Very soon, it helps us understand that we are enough. Inside lie all the answers we're looking towards finding outside, and seeking to go out and pursue becomes pointless.

When our hearts are beginning to open once more, remember that this road does not lead to perfection but rather one that leads to authenticity. It doesn't promise certainty or a life free of difficulty. It offers us so much more than that: the courage that comes with the possibility that we will endure life's vagaries… the bravery to embrace our failings… the strength to walk ahead with the sanctity of our beliefs. Living in our hearts means living in the fog of the messiness of being human, allowing ourselves to feel to the fullest, and showing up in the world full out when the way forward appears as a hazy unknown. So, if we do heart, then we return to ourselves. We no longer seek validation outside of ourselves and feel the need to fit ourselves into boxes crafted by other people. We stop the againstness — it's a flow of life, and somewhere on the journey, we know where we are supposed to arrive. To come home to ourselves is to accept all we are: the positive and the challenging, the joy and the sadness, the strong and the weak. It means being honorable to our path not only for where it can lead us and the way in which we can take it but for who it allows us to be along the way.

This homecoming doesn't just change our relationship with ourselves; it changes how we relate to everybody. It's a deeper, more vibrant living while being present, caring, and authentic in our relationships. We have gotten past shticks of hiding behind masks or walls because we know we're enough without them. We are open to welcoming more profound connections; we love and let be loved in ways that suit healing, being seen, and seeing the other. Loving reassures us that our separations are temporary if not an illusion, and it's in these threads of knowing our shared humanity and the sacred that we find belonging and purpose.

Living from our hearts also cannot be about owning our individuality and what we contribute to this world. It means honoring the truth that we have something worthy to contribute by showing up as we are. This is the wisdom of our heart, which tells us how we choose to live, deliberately in our values and what we choose, the things that bring us joy and help us feel fulfilled. It reminds us that our life doesn't have to mirror anybody else's and that our worth isn't tied up in our achievements or what others say about us. When we listen to the voice of our heart, we are stepping into a life of our own making, a life that expresses the elegant, inexorable magnificence of being.

In that lies what will be needed: the ultimate truth. Our heart knows, in its wisdom, that it is loving. Loving is who we are and what connects all of us through every moment, relationship, and choice. This state of being is neither just an emotion nor merely an action. It is a state of being that emanates into our thinking, speaking, and doing, determined by our choice: our heart. Embrace our loving heart. Be with others, especially those closest to us, and express loving through the chaos it might bring. Loving throughout a lifetime reveals beauty in disarray. Going home to ourselves is not a one-time act but a lifelong practice. We'll experience moments when we are deeply connected to our heart's wisdom and times when we feel completely lost or disconnected. That's part of the journey. So, should we wander a bit, we can always return. It's there waiting for us with open arms and a patient reminder of who we are and what truly matters. Have faith in what it knows.

References

1. Adair, J. (1990). How to Grow Leaders: The Seven Key Principles of Effective Leadership Development. London: Kogan Page.

2. Adler, R. B., & Elmhorst, J. M. (2016). Communicating at Work: Strategies for Success in Business and the Professions (11th ed.). New York: McGraw-Hill Education.

3. Allen, T. D., & Eby, L. T. (2007). The Blackwell Handbook of Mentoring: A Multiple Perspectives Approach. Malden, MA: Blackwell Publishing.

4. American Psychiatric Association. (2013). Diagnostic and Statistical Manual of Mental Disorders (DSM-5). American Psychiatric Publishing.

5. Argyris, C., & Schön, D. A. (1978). Organizational Learning: A Theory of Action Perspective. Reading, MA: Addison-Wesley.

6. Baker, W. E., & Sinkula, J. M. (2005). Environmental, Market, and Organizational Factors Influencing the Effectiveness of the Technology Transfer Process. In Journal of Business Research, 58(5), 652-661.

7. Baldoni, J. (2013). The Leaders Guide to Influence: How to Use the Power of Persuasion to Lead Effectively. New York: McGraw-Hill Education.

8. Bennis, W. (2009). On Becoming a Leader. New York: Basic Books.

9. Bennis, W., & Nanus, B. (1997). Leaders: Strategies for Taking Charge. New York: HarperBusiness.

10. Blanchard, K., & Peale, N. V. (1988). The Power of Ethical Management. New York: William Morrow.

11. Bohm, D. (1996). On Dialogue. New York: Routledge.

12. Breines, J. G., & Chen, S. (2012). Self-compassion increases self-improvement motivation. Personality and Social Psychology Bulletin, 38(9), 1133–1143.

13. Brewin, C. R., & Holmes, E. A. (2003). Psychological Foundations of Posttraumatic Stress Disorder. In Psychological Bulletin, 129(5), 746-769.

14. Brouwer, M., & Jansen, P. (2016). The Role of Communication in Leadership Development: A Systematic Review. In Leadership & Organization Development Journal, 37(6), 745-763.

15. Brown, B. (2010). The Gifts of Imperfection: Let Go of Who You Think You're Supposed to Be and Embrace Who You Are. Hazelden Publishing.

16. Brown, Brené (2012). Daring Greatly: How the Courage to Be Vulnerable Transforms the Way We Live, Love, Parent, and Lead. Gotham Books.

17. Brown, Brené (2018). Dare to Lead: Brave Work. Tough Conversations. Whole Hearts. New York: Random House.

18. Brown, M. E., & Treviño, L. K. (2006). Ethical Leadership: A Review and Future Directions. In The Leadership Quarterly, 17(6), 595-616.

19. Brown, M. E., Treviño, L. K., & Harrison, D. A. (2005). Ethical Leadership: A Review and Future Directions. In The Leadership Quarterly, 16(6), 855-886.

20. Bryman, A. (1992). Charismatic Leadership in Business and Organizations. In The Leadership Quarterly, 3(2), 205-218.

21. Brynjolfsson, E., & McAfee, A. (2014). The Second Machine Age: Work, Progress, and Prosperity in a Time of Brilliant Technologies. New York: W.W. Norton & Company.

22. Bryson, J. M. (2018). Strategic Planning for Public and Nonprofit Organizations: A Guide to Strengthening and Sustaining Organizational Achievement. San Francisco: Jossey-Bass.

23. Buchanan, B. (2004). The Role of Trust in Leadership: A New Perspective. In The Leadership Quarterly, 15(1), 115-130.

24. Cameron, K. S., & Quinn, R. E. (2011). Diagnosing and Changing Organizational Culture: Based on the Competing Values Framework. Upper Saddle River, NJ: Pearson Education.

25. Campbell, W. K., & Foster, C. A. (2007). The narcissistic self: Background, an extended agency model, and ongoing controversies. In C. Sedikides & S. Spencer (Eds.), The Self (pp. 115–138). Psychology Press.

26. Catalyst. (2020). *Why Diversity and Inclusion Matter: Quick Take.*

27. Catalyst. (2020). *The Key to Inclusive Leadership.* Retrieved from Catalyst.org.

28. Cherniss, C., & Goleman, D. (2001). The Emotionally Intelligent Workplace: How to Select for, Measure, and Improve Emotional Intelligence in Individuals, Groups, and Organizations. San Francisco: Jossey-Bass.

29. Ciulla, J. B. (2004). Ethics, our heart of Leadership. Westport, CT: Praeger Publishers.

30. Cloud, H., & Townsend, J. (1992). Boundaries: When to Say Yes, How to Say No to Take Control of Your Life. Zondervan.

31. Clutterbuck, D. (2004). Everyone Needs a Mentor: Fostering Talent in Your Organization. London: Chartered Institute of Personnel and Development.

32. Collins, J. C., & Porras, J. I. (1994). Built to Last: Successful Habits of Visionary Companies. New York: HarperBusiness.

33. Coutu, D. L. (2002). How Resilience Works. In Harvard Business Review, 80(5), 46-55.

34. Covey, S. R. (2004). The 7 Habits of Highly Effective People: Powerful Lessons in Personal Change. New York: Simon & Schuster.

35. Covey, S. R. (2006). The Speed of Trust: The One Thing That Changes Everything. New York: Free Press.

36. Cox, T. H., & Blake, S. (1991). Managing Cultural Diversity: Implications for Organizational Competitiveness. In The Executive, 5(3), 45-56.

37. Davenport, T. H., & Prusak, L. (1998). Working Knowledge: How Organizations Manage What They Know. Boston: Harvard Business School Press.

38. Day, D. V., & Halpin, S. M. (2004). Leadership Development: A Review of the Literature. In The Leadership Quarterly, 15(4), 427-450.

39. Deci, E. L., & Ryan, R. M. (2000). The what and why of goal pursuits: Human needs and the self-determination of behavior. Psychological Inquiry, 11(4), 227–268.

40. Deloitte. (2018). The Diversity and Inclusion Revolution: Eight Powerful Truths.

41. Deming, W. E. (1986). Out of the Crisis. Cambridge, MA: Massachusetts Institute of Technology.

42. Dewey, J. (1938). Experience and Education. Macmillan.

43. Dirks, K. T., & Ferrin, D. L. (2002). Trust in Leadership: Meta-Analytic Findings and Implications for Research and Practice. In Journal of Applied Psychology, 87(4), 611-628.

44. Duffy, M. (2020). Making Sense of Organizational Behavior. SAGE Publications.

45. Dweck, C. S. (2006). Mindset: The New Psychology of Success. Random House.

46. Edmondson, A. C. (1999). Psychological safety and learning behavior in work teams. *Administrative Science Quarterly,* 44(2), 350–383.

47. Edmondson, A. C. (2019). The Fearless Organization: Creating Psychological Safety in the Workplace for Learning, Innovation, and Growth. Wiley.

48. Emmons, R. A., & McCullough, M. E. (2003). The psychology of gratitude. Oxford University Press.

49. Fletcher, D., & Sarkar, M. (2013). Psychological Resilience: A Review of the Literature and Implications for Sports Sciences. In Sports Medicine, 43(3), 241-253.

50. Forgas, J. P. (1995). Mood and judgment: The affect infusion model (AIM). *Psychological Bulletin, 117*(1), 39–66.

51. Frankl, V. E. (1946). Man's Search for Meaning. Beacon Press.

52. Fullan, M. (2001). Leading in a Culture of Change. San Francisco: Jossey-Bass.

53. Gardner, H. (1995). Leading Minds: An Anatomy of Leadership. New York: Basic Books.

54. Gibson, S. K., & Gondal, S. (2006). The Importance of Mentoring for Professional Development: A Review of the Current Literature. In The Journal of Leadership Studies, 1(3), 54-65.

55. Gilbert, P. (2010). Compassion Focused Therapy: Distinctive Features. Routledge.

56. Gini, A. (1998). Moral Leadership. In Business Ethics Quarterly, 8(1), 3-20.

57. Goldsmith, M. (2007). What Got You Here Won't Get You There: How Successful People Become Even More Successful. New York: Hyperion.

58. Goleman, D. (1995). Emotional Intelligence: Why It Can Matter More Than IQ. New York: Bantam Books.

59. Goleman, D. (1998). Working with Emotional Intelligence. New York: Bantam Books.

60. Goleman, D. (2000). Leadership That Gets Results. Harvard Business Review.

61. Goleman, D. (2000). The New Leaders: Transforming the Art of Leadership into the Science of Results. London: Little, Brown and Company.

62. Goleman, D. (2013). Focus: The Hidden Driver of Excellence. New York: HarperCollins.

63. Gonzalez, J. A., & DeNisi, A. S. (2009). Cross-Level Effects of Diversity on Performance: The Role of Team Leader Gender. In The Leadership Quarterly, 20(1), 15-26.

64. Hackman, J. R., & Johnson, C. E. (2009). Leadership: A Communication Perspective (5th ed.). Long Grove, IL: Waveland Press.

65. Hamel, G., & Prahalad, C. K. (1994). Competing for the Future. Boston: Harvard Business School Press.

66. Hargrove, R. (2002). Mastering the Art of Leadership: A Comprehensive Guide to Leadership Development. New York: St. Martin's Press.

67. Hay, L. (1984). You Can Heal Your Life. Hay House

68. Heath, C., & Heath, D. (2007). Made to Stick: Why Some Ideas Survive and Others Die. New York: Random House.

69. Heen, S., & Stone, D. (2014). *Thanks for the Feedback: The Science and Art of Receiving Feedback Well.* Viking.

70. Heifetz, R. A. (1994). Leadership Without Easy Answers. Cambridge, MA: Harvard University Press.

71. Heifetz, R. A., & Laurie, D. L. (1997). The Work of Leadership. In Harvard Business Review, 75(1), 124-134.

72. Hernandez, M. (2012). Toward an Understanding of the Leadership Legacy: A Conceptual Framework. In Leadership & Organization Development Journal, 33(6), 532-548.

73. Hewlett, S. A., Marshall, M., & Sherbin, L. (2011). How Diversity Can Drive Innovation. In Harvard Business Review, 89(2), 30-32.

74. Higgins, M. C., & Kram, K. E. (2001). Reconceptualizing Mentoring at Work: A Developmental Network Perspective. In The Academy of Management Review, 26(2), 264-288.

75. Hunt, J. G., & Conger, J. A. (1999). Leadership in Organizations (2nd ed.). Upper Saddle River, NJ: Prentice Hall.

76. Hunt, V., Layton, D., & Prince, S. (2015). Why Diversity Matters: The Economic Case for Diversity in the Workplace. McKinsey & Company.

77. Kahn, W. A. (1990). Psychological Conditions of Personal Engagement and Disengagement at Work. In Academy of Management Journal, 33(4), 692-724.

78. Kahneman, D. (2011). Thinking, Fast and Slow. New York: Farrar, Straus and Giroux.

79. Kane, G. C., Palmer, D., Phillips, A. N., & Kiron, D. (2015). Strategy, Not Technology, Drives Digital Transformation. In MIT Sloan Management Review.

80. Kant, I. (1781). *Critique of Pure Reason.* (Translated by N. Kemp Smith, 1929). Macmillan.

81. Kant, I. (1785). Groundwork of the Metaphysics of Morals. Cambridge: Cambridge University Press.

82. Kaplan, R. S., & Norton, D. P. (1996). The Balanced Scorecard: Translating Strategy into Action. Boston: Harvard Business School Press.

83. Kellett, J. B., Humphrey, R. H., & Sleeth, R. G. (2006). Empathy and Leadership: An Emerging Perspective. In The Leadership Quarterly, 17(2), 146-162.

84. Kerns, C. D. (2003). Creating a Culture of Trust: The Role of Ethical Leadership. In The Journal of Leadership Studies, 9(1), 36-47.

85. Khoshaba, D. (2012). Self-love and what it means. Psychology Today.

86. Kirkpatrick, D. L. (1994). Evaluating Training Programs: The Four Levels. San Francisco: Berrett-Koehler Publishers.

87. Kirkpatrick, D. L., & Kirkpatrick, J. D. (2006). Evaluating Training Programs: The Four Levels (3rd ed.). San Francisco: Berrett-Koehler Publishers.

88. Kotter, J. P. (1996). Leading Change. Boston: Harvard Business Review Press.

89. Kouzes, J. M., & Posner, B. Z. (2017). *The Leadership Challenge: How to Make Extraordinary Things Happen in Organizations.* San Francisco: Jossey-Bass.

90. Kram, K. E. (1985). Mentoring at Work: Developmental Relationships in Organizational Life. Glenview, IL: Scott, Foresman.

91. Kurtz, S. M., & Almeder, L. (2005). The Importance of Empathy in Communication. In Health Communication, 18(1), 1-10.

92. Lencioni, P. (2002). The Five Dysfunctions of a Team: A Leadership Fable. San Francisco: Jossey-Bass.

93. Lichtenstein, B. M. B., & D. L. (2006). The Challenge of Leading Change: A Study of Organizational Change in the 21st Century. In The Leadership Quarterly, 17(5), 556-578.

94. Luthans, F., & Avolio, B. J. (2003). Authentic Leadership Development. In Positive Organizational Scholarship: Foundations of a New Discipline. San Francisco: Berrett-Koehler.

95. Luthans, F., & Youssef, C. M. (2007). Emerging Positive Organizational Behavior. In Journal of Management, 33(3), 321-349.

96. Masten, A. S. (2001). Ordinary Magic: Resilience Processes in Development. In American Psychologist, 56(3), 227-238.

97. Mayer, R. C., Davis, J. H., & Schoorman, F. D. (1995). An Integrative Model of Organizational Trust. In Academy of Management Review, 20(3), 709-734.

98. Mintzberg, H. (1994). The Rise and Fall of Strategic Planning. New York: Free Press.

99. Neff, K. (2003). Self-compassion: An alternative conceptualization of a healthy attitude toward oneself. Self and Identity, 2(2), 85–101.

100. Neff, K. (2011). Self-Compassion: The Proven Power of Being Kind to Yourself. HarperCollins.

101. Neff, K., & Germer, C. K. (2013). A pilot study and randomized controlled trial of the mindful self-compassion program. Journal of Clinical Psychology, 69(1), 28–44.

102. Neff, K., & Vonk, R. (2009). Self-compassion versus global self-esteem: Two different ways of relating to oneself. Journal of Personality, 77(1), 23–50.

103. Nietzsche, F. (1886). *Beyond Good and Evil.* (Translated by W. Kaufmann, 1966). Random House.

104. Nishii, L. H., & Özbilgin, M. F. (2007). Global Diversity Management: An Evidence-Based Approach. In International Journal of Human Resource Management, 18(2), 111-130.

105. Noe, R. A. (1988). An Investigation of the Determinants of Successful Assigned Mentoring Relationships. In Personnel Psychology, 41(3), 457-479.

106. Northouse, P. G. (2018). Leadership: Theory and Practice (8th ed.). Thousand Oaks, CA: Sage Publications.

107. Page, S. E. (2007). The Difference: How the Power of Diversity Creates Better Groups, Firms, Schools, and Societies. Princeton, NJ: Princeton University Press.

108. Porter, M. E. (1996). What Is Strategy? In Harvard Business Review, 74(6), 61-78.

109. Ragins, B. R., & Kram, K. E. (2007). The Handbook of Mentoring at Work: Theory, Research, and Practice. Thousand Oaks, CA: Sage Publications.

110. Reich, W. (2014). Resilience: Hard-Won Wisdom for Living a Better Life. New York: HarperCollins.

111. Roberson, Q. M. (2006). Disentangling the Meanings of Diversity and Inclusion in Organizations. In Group & Organization Management, 31(2), 212-236.

112. Rogers, C. R. (1980). A Way of Being. Boston: Houghton Mifflin.

113. Rogers, E. M. (2003). Diffusion of Innovations (5th ed.). New York: Free Press.

114. Rost, J. C. (1991). Leadership for the Twenty-First Century. Westport, CT: Praeger.

115. Schacter, D. L., Gilbert, D. T., & Wegner, D. M. (2011). *Psychology.* Worth Publishers.

116. Schein, E. H. (2010). Organizational Culture and Leadership (4th ed.). San Francisco: Jossey-Bass.

117. Schmidt, E., & Rosenberg, J. (2014). How Google Works. New York: Grand Central Publishing.

118. Seligman, M. E. P. (2011). Flourish: A Visionary New Understanding of Happiness and Well-Being. New York: Free Press.

119. Senge, P. M. (1990). The Fifth Discipline: The Art & Practice of the Learning Organization. New York: Doubleday.

120. Sherman, D. K., Cohen, . L., & Steele, C. M. (2009). The psychology of self-affirmation: Sustaining the integrity of the self. Advances in Experimental Social Psychology, 38, 183–242.

121. Shin, S. J., & Park, S. (2018). The Role of Diversity in Team Creativity: A Meta-Analytic Review. In Journal of Organizational Behavior, 39(8), 920-935.

122. Sinek, S. (2009). Start with Why: How Great Leaders Inspire Everyone to Take Action. New York: Portfolio.

123. Sosik, J. J., & Godshalk, V. M. (2000). Leadership Styles, Mentoring Functions Received, and Job Related Stress: A Conceptual Model and Preliminary Study. In Journal of Organizational Behavior, 21(8), 865-878.

124. Thomas, D. A., & Ely, R. J. (1996). Making Differences Matter: A New Paradigm for Managing Diversity. In Harvard Business Review, 74(5), 79-90.

125. Trevino, L. K., Hartman, L. P., & Brown, M. E. (2000). Moral Reasoning and Leadership Ethics: A Review and Conceptual Framework. In The Leadership Quarterly, 11(3), 205-224.

126. Ulrich, D., & Lake, D. (1990). Organizational Capability: Competing from the Inside Out. New York: Wiley.

127. Van Kleef, G. A. (2009). How Emotions Regulate Social Life: The Emotions as Social Information (EASI) Model. In Current Directions in Psychological Science, 18(3), 184-188.

128. Wang, C. K. J., & Degroot, J. (2010). The Development of a Resilience Scale for Adolescents. In Journal of Adolescence, 33(2), 329-340.

129. Wertheimer, M. (1923). Laws of organization in perceptual forms. *Psychologische Forschung, 4*(1), 301–350.

130. Zachary, L. J. (2000). The Mentor's Guide: Facilitating Effective Learning Relationships. San Francisco: Jossey-Bass.
131. Zenger, J. H., & Folkman, J. R. (2019). The Extraordinary Leader: Turning Good Managers into Great Leaders. New York: McGraw-Hill Education.

HTTP://www.peoplesavvy.com

About the Author

With a career spanning over four decades, Dr. Stebbins has become a global authority on Wise Leadership, Transcendent Leadership, and Loving Leadership, updating how we choose to lead in the modern era.

Leaders who not only possess the business acumen to navigate the complexities of the corporate world but also have the inner wisdom and awareness to inspire and engage their team on a profound level. That's precisely what Dr. Stebbins aims to cultivate through this groundbreaking book, *Wise Leadership: Embracing Our Heart's Wisdom.*

Dr. Stebbins brings to the market a unique blend of senior business leadership experience and an in-depth understanding of the intricate human dynamics that shape the workplace. With multiple articles and books, he has become a sought-after expert in the field, sharing his insights with organizations across the globe.

His lifelong dedication to personal growth and development sets Dr. Stebbins apart. He holds an impressive array of academic credentials, including a doctoral degree from Pepperdine University's School of Education and Psychology and an MBA in Finance from the University of Southern California. However, it's his deep immersion in Eastern and Western wisdom teachings, coupled with a daily meditation practice spanning over 55 years, that truly fuels his transformative approach to leadership.

Dr. Stebbins' mission is to positively impact the lives of leaders and their organizations by helping them cultivate inner, relational, and organizational wisdom. He teaches that true leadership includes, yet also goes beyond mere tactics and strategies; it requires a fundamental shift in consciousness and a deep connection to one's authentic self. With his guidance, you'll embark on a transformative journey to elevate your professional performance and enrich your personal life in ways you never thought possible. Get ready to lead with wisdom, transcendence, and loving — the future of leadership.